THE BRO_____ APPLE & PEAR RECIPE BOOK

**COMPILED & PUBLISHED BY
GEERINGS OF ASHFORD LTD**

Illustrations by Barbara Seth

ISBN 1 873953 11 9
Designed and printed by Geerings of Ashford Limited
Cobbs Wood House, Chart Road, Ashford, Kent TN23 1EP

BROGDALE

Brogdale, the national fruit trials research station which is home to the National Fruit Collections has developed a world-wide reputation for its work in testing, developing, protecting and promoting fruit.

Its location, close to Faversham in the heart of the Garden of England could hardly be more appropriate. It was at nearby Teynham in the early 16th century that Henry VIII's frutier Richard Harris introduced grafts of the best available apples and pears and established an orchard which laid the foundations for English fruit growing.

Today Brogdale houses a unique collection of fruit. Its 12 hectares contain a staggering 2,200 apple varieties, 550 types of pear, 350 plum varieties, 220 different cherries and 320 bush fruits.

Although they are held principally as a gene bank for the future, the National Fruit Collections are part of our national heritage. The collections date back to the early 1800's, when they were based at the Horticultural Society at Chiswick, and moved to Brogdale in the 1950's.

Brogdale is administered by the Brogdale Horticultural Trust, a private limited company with charitable status, which bought the National Fruit Trials Centre in 1991 when its future was threatened by government spending cuts. HRH The Prince of Wales is the Patron of the Trust and takes a close interest in its work and progress.

In addition to housing the National Fruit Collections, Brogdale continues to provide an independent, impartial evaluation of fruit varieties. These fruit 'trials' began back in 1922 and aim to eliminate confusion between varieties and assess the particular qualities and characteristics of new varieties.

Up to 700 new varieties or selections may be undergoing tests at any time as experts assess characteristics including resistance to disease and pests. New varieties come to Brogdale for testing from all over the world.

The centre's facilities, which include laboratories, propagation facilities and a major modern cold-store, are used for a range of other research and development projects by the Trust, government, supermarkets and other companies.

Among the most important roles of Brogdale today is its development as an educational centre and as a shop window for the public.

Brogdale's visitor centre attracts some 20,000 people a year and expert guides conduct parties through parts of the fruit collection, explaining the fascinating history, folklore and culture of fruit. Throughout the year there are courses and demonstrations dealing with fruit in the garden and, of course, in the kitchen.

APPLES

The relationship between fruit growing and the county of Kent was, perhaps, best summed up by Charles Dickens in The Pickwick Papers, written in the late 1830's.

"Kent, Sir," says his character Jingle. "Everybody knows Kent - apples, cherries, hops and women."

One hundred and seventy years later it can be argued that Kent has far more to offer the world at large than its fruit; and today's Kentish women might feel somewhat insulted at being included on a list of its most desirable produce. But the relationship between Kent and its apples, pears and many other fruits is as strong as ever.

It is only fitting that the National Fruit Research Station is based in the county not far from the site where in around 1500, Richard Harris, fruitier to Henry VIII brought a store of grafts from France, making a significant contribution to the improvement in the quality of apples available in the country.

Yes! Whisper it softly, but the fruit we often think of as being as English as Roast Beef, is not a native of these shores at all.

In fact, it was the Romans who, along with long straight roads, central heating, and public hygiene, brought the apple to Britain in around 55BC.

The modern apple is believed to have originated in South East Asia and, as with so many other things, the Greeks then played their role in the spread of the fruit. As Christianity moved westwards, the apple followed, becoming an important fruit grown in many religious communities.

After the Norman conquest of Britain the monasteries played a critical role in the developments of the apple, although much of the production was of questionable quality because the fruit was produced on trees grown from seed, rather than from grafts.

It was probably just as well that the bulk of the crops went towards cider production.

The number of apple varieties grown in Britain increased greatly in the 19th century thanks to the encouragement of the Royal Horticultural Society and the work of individuals like Thomas Laxton. Laxton, a nurseryman from Bedford, bred new, high quality varieties which were planted commercially.

Julius Caesar, Norman the Conqueror, Harris and Laxton have all played their part in developing the British apple and today there are well over 2,000 apple varieties housed at Brogdale.

The fruit is so popular that most people asked to name a fruit would plump for apple and many would be able to name three or four varieties. That certainly wouldn't be the case with other popular fruit, even the orange.

The fact is that the apple has become more than a mere fruit. It is part of our culture and remains as important an icon today as it was in Biblical times.

The apple, after all, made the earliest possible entry into history with a starring role in the Garden of Eden. But according to American writer Mark Twain, despite the obvious attraction of the fruit, Adam had other things on his mind when he took the fateful bite.

"Adam was but human - this explains it all. He did not want the apple for the apple's sake, he wanted it only because it was forbidden," he wrote in Puddinhead Wilson's Calendar.

So the humble apple - defined in the Concise Oxford Dictionary simply as the round, firm flesh of the apple tree - was there at the very dawn of humankind. Since then it has assumed symbolic significance quite out of proportion to its role as a watery yet simple food: high in carbohydrates, and an excellent source of dietary fibre and vitamins A and C.

After all, the apple is one of the very first objects modern children learn to recognise. And it would be inconceivable that youngsters learning to read should recognise the letter 'A' as being for anchovy rather than for the bright plump red and green apples which illustrate so many alphabet charts.

The apple has also played its role in history. Sir Isaac Newton is said to have come to the opinion what goes up must come down and formulated the laws of gravity when an apple fell on his head while he took a catnap in an orchard.

Elsewhere, the legendary Swiss William Tell demonstrated his prowess with the cross-bow by shooting an apple from his son's head . . . an obviously risky trick seized upon centuries later by the production of the hugely successful television show 'The Golden Shot'.

In language too, the apple has made its mark. You don't have to have been born within earshot of the Bow Bells to recognise "Apples and Pears" as the cockney rhyming slang for stairs, while a person is particularly proud of the "apple of their eye" and a particularly nasty piece of work will always be recognised by the term "rotten apple".

In the U.S.A. there is a particular fascination with the apple. New York City is known throughout the world as 'The Big Apple', - although some would suggest this particular apple is rotten to the core - and the phrase 'Mom's Apple Pie' has come to represent a nostalgia for a particular type of patriotic Americanism, embodying all the virtues of the family, the flag and a way of life which many believe hardly exists today.

References to the Apple are by no means confined to the past. When a group of brilliant young American computer boffins set up a company to produce a massively successful alternative to IBM's PC's they named the company Apple. When the Beatles formed their own recording company in the late 1960's they too decided to name it Apple.

In short, the Apple remains an instantly recognisable icon with essentially healthy connotations; a perfect image for the modern marketing man to work with.

That the apple has assumed such cultural importance should come as no surprise. Each year the world's apple crop averages some 32 million metric tons, with the countries of former Soviet Union, the U.S.A., China, France, Italy, Hungary, Argentina, Cuba and South Africa among the most significant producers.

According to the Guinness Book of Records, the Miklovic family of Michigan, U.S.A. made a good fist of adding to the overall crop all by themselves when they grew a single apple weighing 3lb 2oz (1.43kg) in 1992.

While half the world's apples are eaten as fresh fruit, jams, pie fillings, juices and ciders account for much of the remainder.

The fascinating and imaginative recipes collected in this book have been chosen to introduce you to the full potential of the apple in everyday cooking.

Bon Appetite!

APPLES FOR FLAVOUR

Flavour is a very personal thing. For this reason, any list can only give an indication of flavour based upon long established reputation and the views of knowledgable apple experts. This is how the following guide list has been developed. The traditional accepted eating qualities of the leading dessert cultivars were almost certainly built around the concept of aroma and flavour - to be savoured after dinner, with the port? There are, however, many types of flavoursome eating from the aromatic rich flavour of a Cox through the honeyed quality of a good ripe Golden Delicious and aniseed detected in Ellison's Orange to the nutty, dry taste of Egremont Russet.

Some varieties mentioned will be easily obtained in season from good greengrocers and supermarkets, for others some farm shops can provide a wide range but some will only be available if grown in your own garden. Trees for garden planting are now relatively easily found from specialist suppliers. A wide range of fresh fruit is always available in season, August to Easter, from the Orchard Shop at the Brogdale Horticultural Trust.

APPLES WITH THE QUALITY OF GOOD FLAVOUR
DESSERT APPLES (other than Cox)

T = triploid
* = new or more recent introductions

Variety	Natural Season (months)	For	Against
Adams' Pearmain	12-2	Good cropper	Conical fruit
Ashmead's Kernel	12-1	Good texture	Uncertain cropper
Baker's Delicious*	9	Good appearance	Small fruit, short season
D'Arcy Spice	1-3	Russet	Poor appearance, moderate cropper
Discovery	8-9	Good shelf life	Uncertain cropper, cracked fruits, poor flavour unless ripe
Egremont Russet	10-11	A good russet	Uncertain cropper, bitter pit
Elstar*	12-2	Uniform, good appearance	
Epicure (Laxton's)	9	Earliest fine flavoured apple	Small fruit
Fortune (Laxton's)	9	Good shape and texture	Canker, soft flesh, biennial
Gala*	11-2	Good cropper, excellent texture	Small fruit, flavour fades
Greensleeves	9-10	Heavy cropper	Flavour soon fades
Holstein T	10-12	Large fruits	Poor cropper
James Grieve	9-10	Heavy cropper	Bruises easily, acid unless ripe
Jonagold T*	11-1	Heavy cropper, good texture	Very large fruit
Karmijn de Sonnaville*	10-12	Uniform size	Russet patches
Kidd's Orange Red	11-1	Good cropper	Russet patches, variable fruit size
Lord Hindlip	12-3	Large fruit, good colour	Russet patches
Lord Lambourne	9-10	Heavy cropper, even size fruits	Sticky skin
Merton Charm	9-10	Regular cropper, compact tree	Small fruit, creamy-green skin
Orleans Reinette	11-12	Uniform, good size	Biennial, shrivels easily
Pixie*	12-3	Good keeper	Small fruit
Queen Cox	10-12	Good colour	
Red Cox (Potter)*	10-12	Good colour	
Ribston Pippin T	10-11	Regular cropper	Drops easily, poor skin finish
St Edmund's Pippin (=Early Golden Russet)	9-10	Good russet	Small fruit, uncertain cropper
Spartan	12-2	Good texture	Rather small
Sunset	10-11	Regular cropper	Small fruit
Suntan T*	12-2	Compact tree	Rather acid
William Crump	12-2	Good size, late flowering	Light cropper, grey russet marking

CULINARY APPLES (other than Bramley)

Variety	Natural Season (months)	For	Against
Alderman	10-12	Large fruits	Conical fruit
Blenheim Orange T	10-11	Good dessert also	Biennial, dull skin finish
Encore	12-3	Heavy apple	Moderate cropper
George Neal	8-9	Regular cropper, even size fruit	Coloured skin
Golden Noble	9-12	Round, even fruits	Moderate fruit size only
Grenadier	8-9	Good early size	Biennial tendency, dirty skin
Lord Suffield	8-9	Good early size, compact tree	Conical fruit, canker?
Monarch	11-3	Good appearance	Biennial, brittle wood
Newton Wonder	11-3	Even, medium size	Biennial
Norfolk Beauty	9	Large fruits	Uncertain cropper
Rev W Wilks	9-10	Large fruits	Biennial, coloured skin
Warner's King T	9-11	Large fruits	Canker

PEARS
DESSERT PEARS

Most dessert pears can be used in cooking but will behave very differently when they are ripe compared to being just under ripe. Whilst not all the varieties listed are generally available in shops, some farm shops have a wider range. The most commonly available varieties will be Comice and Conference with increasing amounts of a new variety Concorde. Fortunately these three varieties can be used in most recipes with very good results particularly if the stage of ripeness is correct for a given dish.

Williams Bon Chretien - Ripens late August and can be used until mid-September when picked correctly. Medium to large sized, very juicy, sweet, strong musk flavour.

Onward - Ripens early to mid September and will store into early October. Produces medium sized fruit with creamy white, melting, juicy flesh and an excellent flavour.

Merton Pride - Ripens in early September and has a relatively short season of use. It has a large fruit size with creamy flesh and fine texture which melts in the mouth. Has excellent flavour.

Gorham - Ripens early September and can be used until end of September. Small to medium sized fruit which is juicy with slightly musky flavour. Tends to hold its shape in cooking.

Buerre Hardy - Ripens mid September for use through October. Has medium to large fruit with white tender flesh. It is juicy with a 'rose-water' flavour.

Concorde - Ripens end of September and will store to late November. Medium sized with yellowish flesh and juicy sweet flavour.

Conference - Picks at the end September & will store to late November. Medium sized with yellow melting flesh which is sweet and juicy.

Seckle - Harvests late September and can be used until late November. This small fruit has a very sweet, rich flavour.

Doyenne du Comice - Harvests in early to mid October and can be used from natural storage until late November. Medium to large sized fruit with a creamy white melting flesh which is juicy with rich flavour.

Glou Morceau - Picks in mid October and will store until late January. Fruit is large to medium in size with flesh which is white and smooth with a rich flavour.

CULINARY PEARS

All cooking pears are very firm in texture and require much longer cooking than dessert pears. They do however store naturally for a long period. These varieties are virtually unobtainable in shops these days so in order to try them you would either have to grow your own or visit Brogdale.

Black Worcester - Also known as the Warden pear. Picks in late September/October and can be in season until February. A medium large pear with hard cream flesh which can be gritty.

Catillac - Harvests in late October and will store until April. Large fruited with hard, greenish white flesh.

Uvedale's Saint Germain - Usually harvested in October and will store until February/March. Firm white flesh which is tinged green and is acid.

COLD APPLE SOUP (serves 4-6)

1lb/450g cooking apples (peeled, cored and cut into pieces)
1 large lemon
2pt/1.1 litre fruit stock or water
8oz/225g sugar
Half an inch of cinnamon stick
2 tablespoons semolina

Boil apple in half of the fruit stock or water until very soft. Strain and rub through a sieve. Add the remaining pint of fruit stock or water, the lemon juice, grated lemon rind, sugar and cinnamon. Boil for 10 minutes, stir in the dry semolina and cook for about 30 minutes. Take out cinnamon stick and cool soup in refrigerator.

Alternatively, if you wish to serve the soup as a sweet, use three tablespoonfuls of semolina instead of two.

Recommended variety - Early Victoria/Keswick Codlin

PARSNIP AND APPLE SOUP (serves 4-6)

1oz/25g butter or margarine
1 medium size onion (chopped)
2 medium size parsnips (peeled and chopped)
1 medium size ccoking apple (peeled, cored and chopped)
1pt/575ml vegetable stock
2 tablespoons/30g chopped parsley
Half teaspoon mixed herbs
1pt/575ml milk
Salt & pepper

Melt butter in a large saucepan and sauté the vegetables and apple, stirring frequently, until onion is transparent. Add stock and herbs, bring to the boil and reduce heat. Cover and simmer for 30 minutes. Add the milk. Allow to cool slightly before blending in a liquidizer in small quantities. Reheat to serve and adjust seasoning to taste.

Recommended variety - Early Victoria

APPLE AND PEANUT BUTTER SOUP (serves 6)

2pt/1.1 litre milk
1 medium size ccoking apple (peeled, cored and grated)
4 tablespoons peanut butter
Juice of 1 lemon
3 tablespoons/45g porridge oats
Quarter teaspoon ground ginger
Salt & pepper
Chopped parsley (for garnish)

Heat milk to just below boiling point and add the grated apple. Blend together the peanut butter and lemon juice and add to the milk with the remaining ingredients. Simmer for 15 minutes. Allow to cool slightly and then blend small quantities in a liquidizer. Reheat to serve and adjust seasoning. Sprinkle with chopped parsley.

This soup can be served chilled, if desired.

Recommended variety - Early Victoria/Keswick Codlin

CARROT, APPLE AND CASHEW NUT SOUP (serves 6)

1lb/450g carrots (chopped)
1 large onion (chopped)
1 small potato (chopped)
1 large cooking apple (peeled, cored and chopped)
2oz/50g butter or margarine
2pt/1.1 litre vegetable stock
2oz/50g broken cashew nuts
Salt & pepper

Melt butter or margarine in a large saucepan and sauté the vegetables for 5 minutes stirring occasionally. Add the remaining ingredients, bring to the boil, cover and simmer for 30 minutes until the vegetables are just tender. Allow to cool before blending in a liquidizer in small quantities. Reheat to serving temperature and adjust seasoning to taste.

Recommended variety - White Transparent/Lodi

LOVE APPLE SOUP (serves 4)

1lb/450g tomatoes (skinned and roughly chopped)
6oz/175g carrots (finely chopped)
1 large or 2 small eating apples (peeled, cored and chopped)
1 onion (peeled and finely chopped)
Half ounce/14g butter
2 teaspoons/10ml vegetable oil
2pt/1.1 litre good vegetable stock
2 cloves garlic (peeled and finely chopped)
4 tablespoons/60ml double cream
3 bay leaves
Bouquet garni of thyme and marjoram
Croutons for garnish

Melt butter and oil together and cook the onion and garlic over a low heat for about 15 minutes until onion is soft and transparent. Add the carrot and stir until all the fat has been absorbed, then add the remaining ingredients (except for the cream and croutons). Bring to the boil, then cover with a lid and simmer for 45 minutes. Discard the herbs and pass the soup through a sieve, or liquidise, until smooth. Season to taste. Return to a clean pan and reheat but do not allow to boil. Serve with a swirl of cream and croutons. Alternatively use chopped chives or a parsley sprig to garnish.

Recommended variety - White Transparent

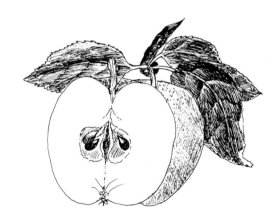

PARSNIP AND PEAR SOUP (serves 4)

12oz/350g parsnips (peeled, halved, cored and chopped)
2 tablespoons/30ml olive oil
1 onion (peeled and chopped)
1 garlic clove (peeled and crushed)
8oz/225g pears (peeled, cored and chopped - reserving 8 slices tossed in the lemon juice)
1 tablespoon/15ml lemon juice
1 pint/575ml vegetable stock
8fl.oz/250ml milk
Ground black pepper
2 tablespoons freshly chopped chives

Heat the oil in a large pan and sauté the parsnips, onion and garlic for 5 minutes. Add the pears, stir in the stock and milk, season and bring to the boil. Reduce the heat and leave to simmer for 20 minutes or until the parsnips are softened. Blend the mixture through a food processor or blender for 2-3 minutes until smooth. Return to the pan, stir in the chives and heat through. Serve garnished with the reserved pear slices.

Recommended variety - Conference

MIXED FRUIT SOUP (serves 4-6)

1 large apple (washed, peeled, cored and chopped into small pieces)
1 large pear (washed, peeled, cored and chopped into small pieces)
1 orange (peeled and chopped into small pieces)
Grated rind and juice of 1 lemon
Any other fruit - strawberries, cherries, etc.
8oz/225g soft brown sugar
1oz/25g cornflour
2pt/1.1 litre fruit stock or water
A few ratafia biscuits

Put prepared fruit into the fruit stock or water and cook until soft. Add the lemon juice and rind and sugar. Add the juice of another lemon or orange if the mixture does not taste fruity enough. Bring back to the boil. Mix the cornflour with 2 tablespoons/130ml of cold water and add to the boiling soup, stirring all the time. Boil for a further 5 minutes; if the cornflour still tastes boil for a few more minutes. Leave to cool and store in a refrigerator until needed. Serve with the ratafia biscuits.

NB. If prepared with a little less water this can be used as a dessert.

Recommended variety - Comice/Merton Pride

APPLE AND RADISH SALAD

2 sharp tasting apples
20 large radishes
8oz/225g Derby Sage or Cheddar cheese
4 tablespoons olive oil
1 dessertspoon Meaux or French mustard

Chop the apples, radishes and cheese into even-sized pieces. Gradually blend oil with the mustard, season and mix the dressing into the salad.

Recommended variety - Newton Wonder

APPLE AND KIPPER SALAD

4 kipper fillets
Juice of 2 lemons
4 sharp tasting apples (peeled, cored and finely diced)
2 tablespoons/30ml horseradish sauce

Skin and dice the fish and soak it in the lemon juice for at least an hour. Mix the diced apples with the kippers and lemon juice and stir in the horseradish sauce. Garnish with cress and serve with brown bread.

Recommended variety - Charles Ross

STUFFED APPLE SALAD

4 even sized apples (wiped and polished)
2 sticks of celery (from the inside of celery head, shredded finely and placed in a bowl of ice-cold water)
2 tablepoons/30ml cream
1 dessertspoon/10ml lemon juice or wine vinegar
A little caster sugar
Ground black pepper
Garlic crushed with salt (optional)
4 walnut halves

Cut off tops of apples and carefully scoop out flesh without breaking the skins. Remove cores and seeds, chop the flesh and place in a bowl. Drain and dry shredded celery, add to the chopped apple and mix well. Blend cream, lemon juice or wine vinegar, sugar and seasoning together (do not stir too vigorously as mixture may curdle) and pour over the apple and celery mix. Stir carefully until fruit is well coated with dressing and then spoon mixture into apple cases and decorate with walnut half.

Recommended variety - Cox's Orange Pippin/Ribston Pippin/Blenheim Orange/Suntan

FENNEL, APPLE AND WALNUT SALAD (serves 4-6)

2 small heads/8oz/225g fennel (halved lengthways)
4 small dessert apples (quartered, cored and thinly sliced)
2oz/50g walnuts (coarsely chopped)
Quarter pint/150ml thick mayonnaise
5 tablespoons/90ml fresh orange juice
Salt and pepper

Trim the feathery green leaves from the fennel tops and reserve for garnish.
Slice the fennel very finely and place in a large bowl. Add the apples and nuts
and stir well to mix thoroughly.

Put mayonnaise in a bowl, add the orange juice and beat until smooth and
thoroughly blended. Season to taste. Pour this dressing over the fennel and
apple and toss until all the ingredients are thoroughly coated. Garnish with
fennel leaves.

Ideal as a side salad with cold roast meat or poultry or with French bread and
cheese for a light supper.

Recommended variety - mix varieties to add colour - Cox/Spartan/Worcester
Pearmain/Granny Smith/Golden Delicious

RED CABBAGE AND APPLE SALAD (serves 6-8)

1¹/4lb/550g red cabbage
3 eating apples (quartered, cored and sliced thinly)
5 tablespoons/75ml French dressing
1 teaspoon/5ml prepared mustard
Half box mustard and cress for garnish

Toss the apple quickly in the dressing to preserve the colour, add the mustard
and mix well. Discard any tough stalks or outside leave of the cabbage and
shred finely. Add to the apple mixture and toss lightly. Pile into a salad bowl
and garnish with cress before serving.

Recommended variety - Granny Smith/Worcester Pearmain

PORK, APPLE AND DANDELION SALAD (serves 4 as a light meal)

12oz/350g cold roast pork (diced into 1¹/2cm/half inch pieces)
1 large cooking apple (cored and chopped into same size pieces)
4 tablespoons/60ml dandelion leaves (chopped)
6 large sage leaves (chopped)
3 tablespoons/45ml cider vinegar
2 tablespoons/30ml sunflower oil
Quarter teaspoon mustard powder
Freshly ground black pepper
Pinch salt

Put pork, apple, dandelion leaves and sage into a bowl. Beat the remaining ingredients together and fold them into the mixture.

Recommended variety - Newton Wonder

CELERY AND APPLE BOATS

8 sticks of celery (wide bottom parts)
2 large cooking apples (peeled, cored and cut into quarter inch/6mm cubes)
4oz/100g curd cheese
2 tablespoons/30ml chopped walnuts

Mix the apples with the cheese. Pile the mixture into the celery sticks and scatter the chopped walnuts over the top.

Recommended variety - Worcester Pearmain/Spartan/Cox

APPLE & HERRING SALAD (serves 2) - Suitable for diabetics

2-3 roll mop herrings
2 large dessert apples (cored but not peeled)
1 small onion
Quarter pint/150ml soured cream

Cut herrings into 1"/25mm pieces, cut apples into thin slices and slice the onion into rings. Mix the herrings, apples and onion together. Put into dish and pour over soured cream.

Recommended variety - Cox

MELON AND APPLE COCKTAIL (serves 10)

3lb/1350g honeydew melon
1lb/450g red eating apples (wiped, quartered and cored)
Juice of 1 large lemon
Half pint/250ml lemonade

Cut melon into quarters, scoop out pips, and cut each quarter in half. With a small sharp knife, cut the flesh away from the skin in one piece then cut it into cubes and put into a bowl.

Slice apples thinly into a basin with the lemon juice, and toss carefully to coat. Add to the melon and pour over the lemonade. Cover and leave the fruit until it is required.

Spoon into serving glasses up to 4 hours before serving.

NB. The melon can be prepared overnight. Cover the basin with cling film and leave in the least cold place in the fridge.

PEARS IN SALADS

Pears used in salads make a tasty and interesting alternative to apples.

Peel, core and slice a ripe well-flavoured dessert pear and dress with a lemon-based dressing and serve on a bed of lettuce. Alternatively, season sliced pears with sugar and lemon juice and chopped fresh mint.

Pears diced and mixed with equal quantities of cucumber and pineapple, cucumber and grapes, or cucumber and melon, dressed with a vinaigrette make a refreshing starter.

Various cheeses can make further alternatives using Roquefort, Brie, Stilton or crumbly English cheeses such as Cheshire and Lancashire. Peel, halve and core the pears and stuff with a mixture of cheese and cream and served with a creamy dressing on a base of lettuce leaves. Alternatively the cheese can be mashed into a vinaigrette and poured over sliced pears.

Recommended varieties for salads - Comice or Conference and they must be ripe.

PEARS WITH ROQUEFORT DRESSING

4 large firm, ripe pears lightly chilled (peeled, halved, cored and sliced)
Lemon juice
Lettuce leaves
Walnuts or pecan nuts to garnish

Dressing -
2oz/50g Roquefort cheese (crumbled)
Quarter pint/150ml thick lemon mayonnaise (preferably homemade)
2 tablespoons/30ml lightly whipped double cream
Salt

Sprinkle sliced pears with lemon juice and arrange on a bed of lettuce leaves on a serving dish. Make the dressing by beating the cheese into the mayonnaise and folding in the cream. Add more seasoning if desired. Spoon dressing over pears and garnish with nuts.

PEARS IN TARRAGON DRESSING

4 firm pears (peeled, cored and chopped)
4 tablespoons/60ml double cream
1 dessertspoon tarragon mustard*
1 dessertspoon wine vinegar*
8 large lettuce leaves
2oz/50g chopped walnuts
*Alternatively you can use tarragon vinegar and Dijon mustard

Blend the mustard and cream and beat in the vinegar. Arrange the lettuce leaves on a dish, pile pears on top and coat with the dressing. Garnish with the walnuts.

Recommended variety - Conference

PEARS IN TARRAGON CREAM DRESSING

3-4 pears (peeled, halved and cored)
Lettuce leaves
Paprika

Dressing-
1 egg
2oz/50g caster sugar
3 tablespoons/45ml tarragon vinegar
Salt & pepper
Quarter pint/150ml double cream

To make the dressing, beat egg in a bowl, add the sugar and gradually add the vinegar. Stand bowl in a pan of boiling water and stir until the mixture begins to thicken. Remove from heat and continue to stir. When mixture resembles thick cream, take basin out of pan and stir for a few more seconds. Season lightly and leave until cold. Lightly whip the cream and fold into the dressing.

Arrange halved pears, rounded side up, each on a lettuce leaf on individual serving plates, coat each with one tablespoon of the dressing and sprinkle over a little paprika.

Recommended variety - Comice

PEAR AND CURD CHEESE SALAD

4 firm pears (peeled and cut in half lengthways)
4oz/100g curd cheese
Juice of 1 lemon
2 tablespoons chopped fresh cob nuts

Discard the cores of the pears and then scoop out enough flesh to leave quarter-inch/6mm deep cups. Chop the scooped out flesh, brush the shells with lemon juice and blend the remaining juice with the cheese mixing the chopped pears. Pile back into the pear cups and sprinkle over the chopped nuts. Serve immediately.

Recommended variety - Conference

PEAR AND HAM SALAD (serves 4)

4 small firm pears (peeled and cut into slices 2" x 1/2"/ 5cm x 11/4cm)
3oz/75g lean ham (finely diced)
4 spring onions (using the bulbs only) or 1 small onion (chopped)
4oz/100g curd cheese
2 tablespoons/30ml sour cream
Juice of 1 lemon

Coat the pear slices with the lemon juice. Mix the ham and onions with the cheese and cream. Pile mixture onto four small plates (or one large one if preferred) using a base of lettuce or cress if desired and garnish with the pear slices. Top with a sprig of parsley.

Recommended variety - Conference

PEARS WITH STILTON (serves 4)

3oz/75g stilton cheese
3oz/75g cream cheese
4 large ripe dessert pears (washed and cored)
Juice of 1 lemon
4 fresh mint sprigs to garnish

Dressing -
3 tablespoons/45ml olive oil
1 tablespoon/15ml lemon juice
1 tablespoon chopped fresh mint
1 teaspoon sugar
Salt & ground black pepper

Coat the inside of each pear with the lemon juice to prevent discolouration.

Beat together the stilton and cream cheese until soft and spoon into a piping bag with large plain nozzle. Pipe into the centre of the pears and put in the fridge until ready to serve. To make the dressing put the oil, lemon juice, chopped mint, sugar, salt and pepper in a jar with a tight fitting lid and shake vigorously, adjusting the seasoning to taste.

To serve, slice each pear across in round slices, arrange on a serving plate and spoon over the dressing. Garnish with mint sprigs.

Recommended variety - Comice

PEAR, WALNUT AND CELERY SALAD

2 large ripe pears (washed, halved and cored)
2oz/50g chopped walnuts
1 teacup finely chopped celery
8oz/225g cream cheese
1 tablespoon/15ml mayonnaise

Mix walnuts, celery, cream cheese and mayonnaise thoroughly. Arrange pear halves on a serving dish on a bed of lettuce and fill centres with nut and celery mixture.

Recommended variety - Conference

PEARS WITH LEMON & CREAM CHEESE STUFFING AND RAVIGOTE SAUCE (serves 8 if used as a starter)

4 large ripe pears (peeled, cored and halved)
4oz/100g cream cheese
2 egg yolks
Juice and grated rind of 1 lemon
Salt & freshly ground black pepper
Pinch of ground ginger
4 lettuce leaves
1 grapefruit (peeled and segmented)
1oz/25g toasted flaked almonds

For the Ravigote Sauce -
1oz/25g butter
Half ounce/14g wholemeal flour
2½ fl.oz/60ml water or vegetable stock
2½ fl.oz/60ml single cream
Salt & freshly ground black pepper
2 tablespoons/30ml white wine vinegar
2 tablespoons/30ml white wine
2 mushrooms (sliced)
1 tablespoon shallots or onion (chopped)
1 bay leaf
Cayenne or Tabasco

In a bowl combine the cream cheese, egg yolks and lemon juice and rind. Season and add the ginger. Arrange the lettuce leaves on a serving dish and place pear halves on top, filling the centre of each half with the cream cheese mixture. Decorate round the pears with the grapefruit segments and almonds sprinkled over.

Make the sauce as follows - heat the butter in a pan and stir in the flour. Cook for one minute. Gradually add the water or stock, stirring continuously, and boil for 4 minutes, then whisk in the cream. Simmer for 10 minutes. Season. While the sauce is simmering put the rest of the ingredients into another saucepan and boil briskly until reduced by one-third. Then whisk in the sauce and boil for a further 5 minutes. Strain mixture, check the seasoning and add a pinch of cayenne or tabasco if desired.

Serve with the arranged pears.

Recommended variety - Comice

PEAR AND CHEESE STARTER (serves 4)

4 ripe pears (halved and cored)*
4oz/100g curd cheese
Small lettuce
2 tablspoons/30ml light salad dressing
2oz/50g chopped walnuts
A few finely snipped chives
*If using tinned allow 8 halves and drain well

Scoop out a little of the flesh from the pears. Line a serving dish with lettuce leaves, shredding the remainder and making four hollows. Place pears in hollows and heap in the curd cheese. Spoon over the dressing and scatter with chives and chopped walnuts.

Recommended variety - Comice

BLACK PUDDING GRILLED WITH APPLES (serves 3-4)

1lb/450g Black Pudding
6 sweet apples
Pork fat or olive oil

Slice the pudding into lengths of about 5"/12cm and coat each side with the pork fat or olive oil. Grill for about 5 minutes on each side. Peel, core and slice the apples and gently fry in pork fat. Serve the pudding on the bed of sliced apples. Garnish as desired.

Recommended variety - Charles Ross

HEAVEN AND EARTH (serves 4-6)

2lb/900g of potatoes
Salt and pepper
1lb/450g apples (washed, cored and cut into chunks)
4oz/100g/6 slices fatty smoked bacon (rind removed and chopped)
Chopped parsley

Cut potatoes into large cubes and cook in boiling salted water for about 15 minutes. Drain thoroughly.

Using a heavy based frying pan, heat the bacon over a fairly low heat until the fat runs, then continue to cook until the bacon is crisp. Remove bacon from pan, drain on absorbent kitchen paper, reserve and keep warm. Add the apples and potatoes to the fat remaining in the pan and cook, turn occasionally, until the apples are tender and the potatoes are hot and slightly browned. Season to taste, add the parsley and sprinkle on the crisp bacon. Serve immediately.

Recommended variety - Newton Wonder/Charles Ross/Golden Noble

PEPPERS WITH APPLES (serves 4)

4 large green peppers
1oz/25g margarine, plus extra for greasing
1oz/25g wholemeal flour
8fl.oz/225 ml milk
1 large cooking apple (chopped)
4oz/100g Gruyère cheese (grated)
1 small red pepper (trimmed and chopped)
1 large tomato (sliced thickly)
Salt and pepper
Set oven at 150C/300F/Gas Mark 2.

Cut the tops off the green peppers, discard membranes and seeds but keep tops. Blanch peppers and tops in boiling salted water for 3 minutes. Drain thoroughly.

Melt margarine in a small saucepan, stir in the flour and cook over an gentle heat for 2-3 minutes, stirring constantly. Do not let the flour brown. Take off the heat and add the milk gradually while stirring. Return to the heat, bring to the boil and simmer until the sauce thickens and stir occasionally. Season to taste and stir in the chopped apple, grated cheese and red pepper.

Trim the bases of the green peppers so they stand evenly making sure not to cut through the flesh. Spoon the filling into the peppers, replace tops and place in a lightly greased dish. Cook stuffed peppers for 30 minutes. Garnish with the sliced tomato.

Recommended variety - Peasgood Nonsuch

PORK AND APPLE TERRINE (serves 3-4)

6oz/175g fairly lean pork cut into ¼ inch/6mm cubes
4oz/100g lean bacon also cut into same size cubes
1 small cooking apple diced into same size cubes
1 small onion (finely chopped)
6 sages leaves (chopped)

Set oven at 170C/325F/Gas Mark 3.

Mix the pork, bacon, apple, onion and sage together and press into 1lb/450g terrine dish. Cover and put into the oven for two hours. Remove from oven and set a weight on top until it is cool. Turn out just prior to serving.

Recommended variety - Blenheim Orange

BEEF SAUSAGES WITH APPLE AND TOMATO SAUCE (serves 4)

For the sausages -
1lb/450g coarsely minced good quality beef
1oz/25g butter
1 small onion (finely chopped)
1 clove garlic (finely chopped)
1 teaspoon turmeric
1 teaspoon ground cumin
Half teaspoon ground allspice
Half teaspoon cayenne pepper
1 tablespoon chopped mixed herbs

For the sauce -
1lb/450g cooking apples
2 strips lemon rind
3 ripe tomatoes (skinned and chopped)
1 dessertspoon grated onion

To make the sausages, melt butter on a low heat in a small frying pan and cook the onion and garlic until the onion is transparent. Put meat in a large mixing bowl and beat in the onion mixture, spices, herbs and seasoning. Divide the mixture into eight portions and form into sausage shapes about two inches long and one inch diameter. Preheat the grill to high and grill sausages fairly close to heat until they are brown and crisp all round.

To make the sauce, stew the apples with the lemon rind until they are soft and then sieve them - this should give you about 6 fluid ozs/175ml of purée. Put the purée with the tomatoes and onion into a saucepan and beat them together over a moderate heat until the tomatoes start to go pulpy. Sieve the mixture again to take out the tomato pips. Season, reheat and serve either separately or poured over the sausages.

Recommended variety - Newton Wonder/Charles Ross

HERRINGS WITH BACON AND APPLE SAUCE (serves 4)

4 herrings
Oatmeal to coat

Sauce-
1oz/25g butter
4 rashers lean bacon (diced)
1 large onion (sliced)
1 large cooking apple (peeled, cored and finely chopped)
2 teaspoons of made English mustard
Juice of half a lemon
1 tablespoon chopped thyme or lemon thyme

To make the sauce, melt the butter in a saucepan over a low heat and cook the bacon, onion and apple together until the onion is soft and the apple pulpy. Blend the mustard with the lemon juice and stir into the sauce with the thyme. Season and set aside.

Fillet the herrings and coat in the oatmeal. Grill herrings under a preheated high grill until they are brown. They are an oily fish so will provide their own fat. Serve with the sauce placed in blobs on the top.

Recommended variety - Golden Noble/Charles Ross

HERRINGS WITH CABBAGE AND APPLE (serves 4)

4 herrings
2 tablespoons made English mustard
1 tablespoon chopped thyme or preferably lemon thyme
1oz/25g butter
1 large onion (thinly sliced)
1 large cooking apple (peeled, cored and sliced)
1 small green cabbage (shredded)
Quarter pint/150ml dry cider

Set oven at 180C/350F/Gas Mark 4.

Remove heads, fins and backbones from herrings, keeping them joined down the back. Spread each one fairly thickly with the mustard, sprinkle over with the lemon thyme and reshape herrings. Melt the butter in a heavy flameproof casserole on a low heat and soften the onion and apple slices. Add the cabbage stirring thoroughly to mix all the ingredients and to coat the cabbage well with the butter. Pour in the cider, check the seasoning and bring to the boil. Place the herrings in this mixture and cook in the casserole dish in the oven for 45 minutes.

Recommended variety - Golden Noble/Charles Ross

BRAISED SAVOY CABBAGE IN CIDER (serves 4)

1 Savoy cabbage using inner leaves only (shredded)
1oz/25g butter
1 large cooking apple (thinly sliced)
1 large onion (thinly sliced)
4 tablespoons dry cider
1 tablespoon wine vinegar

Set the oven to 180C/350F/Gas Mark 4.

Blanch the cabbage in boiling salted water for two minutes and drain well. Melt the butter in a casserole on a low heat and cook the apple and onion gently until they are soft. Remove and set aside. Take casserole off heat. Put in a layer of one third of the cabbage, then half the apple and onion mixture, then cabbage, the remaining apple and onion mixture and top with final layer of cabbage. Season. Mix the cider and vinegar and pour into the casserole. Cover and cook in the oven for one hour.

Recommended variety - Lord Derby/Bramley

SAVOY CABBAGE WITH APPLE AND ONION (serves 4)

1 Savoy cabbage using inner leaves only (shredded)
1 large cooking apple (thinly sliced)
1 large onion (thinly sliced)
1oz/25g butter
Quarter pint/150ml stock

Place all the above ingredients in a heavy based saucepan. Season, cover and set on a moderate heat for 20 minutes, stirring occasionally.

Recommended variety - Lord Derby

SAGE AND APPLE POTATOES (serves 4)

4 baked potatoes
2oz/50g butter
12 sage leaves (chopped)
1lb/450g cooking apples (peeled and thinly sliced)

Cut the potatoes in half and scoop out the middles. Mash potato with half the butter and the sage. Put mixture back into the shells, pile the sliced apples on the mixture and dot the remaining butter on the top. Put into a hot oven (220C/425F/Gas Mark 7) for 20 minutes. They are recommended accompanying roast pork.

Recommended variety - Bramley

SAUSAGE AND ONION POPOVERS (serves 4)

5oz/150g plain flour
1pt/575ml milk
1 large cooking apple (peeled and cored)
Dripping or lard for greasing
Half ounce/14g butter
2 eggs
12oz/350g sausage meat
2 onions (skinned and thinly sliced)
1 teaspoon finely chopped fresh parsley

Set the oven to 220C/425F/Gas Mark 7.

Make the batter using 4oz of the plain flour, some of the milk and two eggs.

Break up the sausage meat in a mixing bowl using a fork, grate the apple into it, add seasoning and the parsley. Mix all together and form into 16 small balls. Heat four half pint ovenproof dishes which have been generously greased with dripping or lard until the fat sizzles. Place 4 sausage balls into each dish, cook in the oven for 10-12 minutes, turning once. Pour the batter mixture over the sausage ball and return to the oven for a further 35-40 minutes until the batter is well risen and golden brown.

Make the onion sauce by cooking the onion in the remaining milk until soft. Melt the butter in a pan and stir in the remaining 1oz of flour, cook over a low heat for one minute to blend. Gradually stir in the onion and milk, and bring the the boil and simmer until thickened and continue to stir frequently. Season to taste. To serve, pour a little of the onion sauce in the hollow of the batters as soon as they are cooked. Serve immediately.

Recommended variety - Newton Wonder/Bramley

KENTISH RAREBIT (makes 6 rounds)

2oz/50g butter or margarine
3 dessert apples (peeled, cored and sliced)
12oz/350g Cheddar cheese (grated)
Pepper to taste
Rounds of buttered toast

Melt the butter or margarine in a saucepan, add the apples and cook gently ensuring they do not brown. Add the grated cheese and pepper and mix well together. Spread onto the round of toast and brown under a hot grill until the mixture is bubbling. Serve immediately.

Recommended variety - Golden Noble/Peasgood Nonsuch

CHEESE AND APPLE PIE (serves 4)

6oz/175g shortcrust pastry
1¹/₂lb/675g cooking apples (peeled, cored and sliced)
6oz/175g Cheddar cheese (cut into thin slices)
2oz/50g sugar or to taste
A little water

Set oven at 230C/450F/Gas Mark 8.

Cover the bottom of a 1¹/₂pt/850ml pie dish with a layer of the sliced apples. Sprinkle the sugar evenly on top, cover with the sliced cheese and finish with another layer of apple. Roll out the shortcrust pastry to make a lid for the pie dish. Damp edges of the dish with water and cover with the pastry lid marking the edge with the back of a fork to make a pattern. Place in oven for 10-15 minutes and then reduce heat to 180C/350F/Gas Mark 4 and cook for a further 30 minutes.

Recommended variety - Lord Derby/Bramley

APPLE MARIGOLD (serves 3-4)

3 large cooking apples (peeled, cored and cut into rings)
2 eggs
1 teacupful of milk
1 teaspoon marigold petals
1 teaspoon sweet thyme
1 teaspoon sage
1 small peppercorn (crushed to powder)
Butter

Set oven at 180C/350F/Gas Mark 4.

Beat the eggs in the milk and season with the marigold, thyme, sage and peppercorn. Put mixture in a shallow dish, carefully place apple rings on top with 1 or 2 pieces of butter. Bake for 20-25 minutes.

Recommended variety - Blenheim Orange

APPLE BROWN RICE

6oz/175g cooked brown rice
Half teaspoon salt
Little cooking oil
6oz/175g onions (peeled and thinly sliced)
Teaspoon sugar
Pinch marjoram
8oz/225g apple (unpeeled, quartered and sliced)
Pinch ground cinnamon
Pinch ground cloves
Juice of 1 lemon

Set oven at 180C/350F/Gas Mark 4.

Heat cooking oil and sauté onions with the sugar and marjoram until golden. Toss apples with the cinnamon, cloves and lemon juice. Lightly grease a shallow ovenproof dish and spread half the onions on the bottom, cover with half the rice and then half the apples. Repeat the layers. Bake for about 30 minutes and serve hot garnished with unpeeled slices of red apples dipped in the lemon juice. Ideal served with roast pork, chicken, lamb or pork chops.

Recommended variety - Newton Wonder

BACON AND APPLE HOT POT (serves 4)

1lb8oz/675g collar of bacon
1 level tablespoon/15g cornflour
15fl.oz/425ml stock
2 eating apples (washed, cored and sliced into thick wedges)
2 tablespoons/30ml cooking oil
Half pint/275ml dry cider
1 teaspoon/5ml tomato purée
Black pepper

Leave bacon to soak overnight in cold water to remove excess salt. Drain and cut into 1"/25mm cubes. Heat oil in a large pan and fry the bacon pieces for about 5 minutes. Stir in the cornflour, then gradually add the stock, cider and purée and keep stirring to avoid lumps forming. Season with pepper. Bring to the boil, reduce the heat and keep simmering for about 45 minutes. Add the apple and cook for a further 15 minutes until apple is soft. Serve with jacket or creamed potatoes.

NB. To bring colour to the dish use one red skinned and one green skinned apple.

Recommended varieties - Blenheim Orange/Charles Ross

HUNTINGDON FIDGET PIE (serves 4)

12oz/350g shortcrust pastry
1oz/25g plain flour
8oz/225g back bacon (rinded and roughly chopped)
1 medium onion (skinned and roughly chopped)
8oz/225g apples (peeled, cored and roughly chopped)
1 tablespoon fresh parsley (chopped)
Quarter pint/150ml med.dry cider
1 egg (beaten)

Set oven at 190C/375F/Gas Mark 5.

Mix the bacon, onion and apples in a 1pt/575ml pie dish. Add the parsley and season to taste. Blend the flour with the cider a little at a time and pour into the pie dish. Roll out the pastry, cutting a long thin strip to go around the rim of the pie dish. Moisten rim with a little water and place strip on rim, pressing down lightly. Moisten top of pastry strip and place pastry lid on top, sealing edges, trim and flute the edge. Make a diagonal cross in the centre almost to the edge of the dish and fold pastry back to reveal the filling. Brush pastry with egg and bake for about 45 minutes or until pastry is golden and the filling is cooked. Serve hot with a green vegetable or cold with salad.

NB. Potatoes can be added to the bacon, onion and apple mixture if required.

Recommended variety - Bramley

APPLE SAUERKRAUT

1lb/450g sauerkraut
2oz/50g port fat or butter
3 tart eating apples (washed, quartered and cored)
2 bay leaves
2 onions (skinned and sliced)
4 frankfurter sausages
2 slices bacon
Caraway seeds (optional)
Salt and pepper to taste

Set oven at 190C/375F/Gas Mark 5.

Put sauerkraut in an ovenproof casserole with pork fat or butter, add the apples and then the onion, sausages, bacon, bay leaves and a little water. Cook for about 30 minutes, add seasoning and caraway seeds (if using) and return to oven for a few more minutes. Serve hot.

Recommended variety - Bramley

BRAISED PHEASANT WITH APPLES (serves 4-6)

1 good-sized pheasant
1¹/2oz/40g butter
1 large onion (skinned and chopped)
4 tart apples (cored, peeled and chopped)
1oz/25g flour
Half pint/275ml light stock
4 tablespoons/60ml whisky
4fl.oz/100ml cream (whipping or double)
Salt and pepper to taste
1 green dessert apple, fresh rosemary or watercress

Set oven at 170C/325F/Gas Mark 3.

Brown the pheasant in butter in a heavy pan, transfer to ovenproof casserole and pour over the whisky. Cover and cook for 2 hours or until the bird is very tender.

Put onion and apple in the heavy pan and gently fry until they begin to change colour. Stir in the flour and then the stock. Leave to cool then put through a blender, adjust the seasoning and stir in the cream.

Remove pheasant from casserole, leave to cool and joint the bird, discarding bones and skin and leaving fairly large pieces of meat. Arrange meat in ovenproof dish with a lid, pour over sauce and return to oven for about 20 minutes. Garnish with sections of dessert apple and sprigs of rosemary and watercress. Serve with mushrooms and creamed potatoes.

Recommended variety - Bramley/Blenheim Orange/Newton Wonder

HOTCH POTCH PIE (serves 4)

About 12oz/350g cold cooked pork cut into cubes
Half pint/275ml good stock
1lb/450g cooked potatoes
1oz/25g butter or dripping
4 onions (peeled and boiled until soft)
3 apples (peeled, cored and sliced)
1 med swede (cooked until soft)
A little warmed milk

Set oven at 180C/350F/Gas Mark 4.

Arrange cold meat in bottom of an ovenproof dish. Cover with the onions, season to taste, layer the sliced apple on top and cover with sufficient stock to moisten but not swamp the pie. Mash the potatoes and swede together with the milk and pile on top of pie, covering completely and sealing the edges. Fork a pattern on the top and bake for about an hour when it should be golden brown and the apple cooked. Serve with good rich gravy and green vegetables.

Recommended variety - Bramley/Newton Wonder

PORK CHOPS WITH CRAB APPLE CRUST (serves 4)

4 loin pork chops
12 sage leaves
8oz/225g crab apples (quartered, cored and finely chopped)
1 medium onion (peeled and finely chopped)
2oz/50g fresh wholewheat breadcrumbs
Ground black pepper

Set oven at 200C/400F/Gas Mark 6.

Cut the rind off the chops, leaving most of the fat. Put chops on the rack of a roasting tin and rinds in the tin to render down. Lay two sage leaves on each chop and cook for 45 minutes. While chops are cooking, finely chop remaining sage leaves. Put the onions and chopped apples in a small frying pan. Take 3 tablespoons/45ml of the fat from the roasting tin, pour over onions and apples and cook until the onion is soft. Remove from heat and mix in breadcrumbs, chopped sage and pepper. Spread stuffing mixture over the lean part of the chops and return to oven for a further 15 minutes for the top to brown. Serve the chops plain with no sauce or gravy.

Recommended variety - Veitch's Scarlet

PORK CHOPS IN CIDER SAUCE (serves 4)

4 pork chops
10 sage leaves (chopped)
1 large clove garlic
Quarter teaspoon of salt
Quarter teaspoon ground black pepper
2 large apples (peeled, cored and sliced into rings)
2 teaspoons ground cinnamon

For the sauce -
1 small onion (peeled and finely chopped)
1 small carrot (finely diced)
Half stick celery (finely chopped)
2 tablespoons/30ml olive oil
1 level tablespoon/15g flour
Half pint/275ml dry cider
2 cloves
Small piece of cinnamon

Crush the sage, garlic, salt and pepper together and rub into the chops; leave to stand for four hours.

Cook the vegetables in the oil in a saucepan over a low heat until they are just beginning to brown. Stir in the flour and cook until it browns. Take off the heat and blend in the cider. Return pan to heat and bring sauce gently to the boil and skim if necessary. Add the cloves and cinnamon, cover and simmer very gently for about 30 minutes. Strain it through a sieve, pressing vegetables hard to extract all the juices. Return the sauce to the rinsed pan and simmer for a further five minutes.

Preheat the grill on high. Scrape any pieces of the marinade off the chops and grill under a high heat, turning once until they are completely done and golden brown. When the chops are cooked, lay apple slices on top and sprinkle with the cinnamon. Put back under the hot grill and cook until the apples are done and just beginning to melt into the pork. Arrange the chops on a heated serving dish and pour the sauce over.

Recommended variety - Bramley/Blenheim Orange/Charles Ross

SALT PORK BAKED IN CIDER

2lb8oz/1.1kg piece of salt belly pork with bones
1 carrot (peeled and sliced)
1 onion (peeled and sliced)
1 stick celery (chopped)
Bouquet garni (parsley, thyme & sage)
Few black peppercorns
1 tablespoon/15ml made English mustard
1 tablespoon cloves
2 large apples (peeled, cored and sliced)
Half pint/275ml dry cider

Set oven at 180C/350F/Gas Mark 4.

Put the pork in a pan with the carrot, onion, celery, bouquet garni and peppercorns, bring slowly to the boil and simmer for about an hour, skimming as necessary.

Remove pork from saucepan, peel or cut off rind and take out bones. Spread the top thickly with the mustard and stick in cloves about 1"/25mm apart. Lay pork in an ovenproof dish, place the sliced apple down either side of meat and pour over the cider. Bake for an hour and serve it carved into slices with the apple on top and spooning over any liquid.

Recommended variety - Bramley

PORK AND APPLE PIE (serves 4)

1lb/450g pork
12oz/350g apples (peeled, cored and sliced)
1oz/25g caster sugar
Sage
Salt and black pepper (to taste)
Quarter pint/150ml meat stock
6oz/175g shortcrust pastry
Beaten egg to glaze

Set oven at 190C/375F/Gas Mark 5.

Cut pork into pieces and layer a generous portion at the bottom of a lightly greased pie dish. Season with salt and pepper and sprinkle with a little fresh or dried sage. Place a thin layer of apples on the meat and lightly sprinkle with the sugar. Continue with layers until all ingredients are used and the dish is full. Pour over the stock. Roll out the pastry to make a lid and cover dish, sealing the edges well. Make a slit in the centre to let out the steam and brush with the beaten egg. Bake for one and a half hours and after about 30 minutes or when the pastry is golden brown, lay a sheet of greaseproof paper over the top to prevent burning.

Recommended variety - Bramley/Newton Wonder

PORK KNUCKLES WITH CHESTNUTS AND APPLES (serves 4)

8oz/225g chestnuts (skinned)
2 medium sized apples (peeled, cored and chopped)
2 pork knuckles
2 medium onions (peeled and thinly sliced)
1pint/575ml dry cider
Bouquet garni of parsley, sage, thyme and marjoram
Salt and pepper

Set oven at 180C/350F/Gas Mark 4.

Put the pork knuckles in a large flameproof casserole and surround them with the chestnuts, apples and onions. Pour over the cider, add the bouquet garni and season as desired. Put casserole on a high heat and bring cider the boil. Cover the casserole and put in the oven to cook for one and a half hours. Remove from the oven and take out the pork knuckles, removing the rinds, and carve the meat. Put meat on a heated serving dish and spoon the chestnuts and casserole juices over the top. Serve immediately.

Recommended variety - Bramley/Charles Ross

PORK WITH PUMPKIN AND APPLE SAUCE

2lb/900g rolled shoulder of pork
Half ounce/14g butter
1 medium onion (peeled and sliced)
6oz/175g raw pumpkin (chopped small)
1 medium apple (peeled, cored and sliced)
A bouquet of sage leaves
6 cloves
Quarter pint/150ml stock

Set oven at 180C/350F/Gas Mark 4.

Melt the butter in a heavy flameproof casserole on high heat and brown the joint all over. Remove the meat and lower the heat. Stir in the onion and pumpkin, cover and leave to sweat for 5 minutes. Add the apple to the pan with the sage and cloves, pour over the stock, bring the boil and return the pork to the pan. Cover the casserole and put in the oven for one and half hours. Remove the meat, carve it and keep it warm. Rub all the contents of the casserole through a sieve, reheat the sauce and serve it separately from the meat.

Recommended variety - Bramley

PORK WITH CIDER SUGARED APPLES (serves 4-6)

4lb8oz/2kg loin of pork with skin on
1 pint/575ml dry cider
1 teaspoon red food colouring
6oz/175g granulated sugar
Sprigs of parsley
8 eating apples (peeled and cored)
3 tablespoons vegetable oil
Salt

Set oven at 180C/350F/Gas Mark 4.

Ask your butcher to chine the joint and score the skin. Brush the skin with the oil and sprinkle over the salt to make a crisp crackling. Cook for about two to two and a half hours. Prepare the garnish about 30 minutes before serving. Dissolve the sugar in the cider over a low heat, then bring to the boil, add the colouring and reduce the heat. Poach the apples gently in the cider syrup until they are tender and nicely pink but still whole (about 15-20 minutes). Remove the apples to a plate. Boil the syrup rapidly to reduce to about half the quantity, pour over the apples and leave to set. Serve the pork on a heated dish surrounded by the sugared apples and garnish with a sprig of parsley on each apple.

Recommended variety - Small Cox/Yellow Ingestrie

PORK BONE PIE (serves 6)

1lb8oz/675g pork pieces (these can be from pork left on the bone)
1 large onion (peeled and sliced)
2 apples (peeled, cored and chopped)
1oz/25g good dripping
Quarter pint/150ml stock
Half teaspoon finely chopped thyme
1 egg (beaten)
6oz/175g self-raising flour
4oz/100g cooking lard

Set oven at 200C/400F/Gas Mark 6.

Make a shortcrust pastry by rubbing the lard into the flour with a pinch of salt and adding sufficient cold water to make a pliable, but not sticky, dough. Leave it to rest for 30 minutes.

Brown the pork pieces and onion with a little dripping and transfer to a 1^{1}/2pt/850ml sized pie dish. Add the apples and thyme and pour over the stock. Roll out the pastry to make a lid, seal the edges well, decorate with the spare pastry and brush top with the beaten egg. Cut a couple of slits in the top to allow steam to escape and bake in the pre-heated oven for 30 minutes, then reduce the heat to 170C/325F/Gas Mark 3 and cook for a further 45 minutes. If top is browning too quickly cover lightly with foil or greaseproof paper.

Recommended variety - Bramley

LAMB WITH CRAB APPLE STUFFING (serves 4)

Approx 1^{3}/4lb/800g best end of neck (boned if possible)
3oz/75g crab apples (quartered, cored and finely chopped)
Half ounce/14g butter
1 small onion (peeled and finely chopped)
1 clove garlic (finely chopped)
2oz/50g fresh wholewheat breadcrumbs
1 teaspoon chopped rosemary
4 tablespoons/60ml dry cider

Set oven at 200C/400F/Gas Mark 6.

Melt the butter in a frying pan on a low heat, add the onion and garlic and soften. Remove from heat and mix in breadcrumbs, rosemary, crab apples and cider. Put the stuffing on the cut surface of the lamb, roll it up and tie in about six places with fine cotton string. Place on rack in a roasting tin and cook for 1 hour. Cut into eight slices for serving.

Recommended variety - Veitch's Scarlet/John Downe

MIDWINTER PIE (serves 4-6)

8oz/225g self-raising flour
Pinch of salt
1 large or 2 small apples (peeled, cored and sliced)
6 ripe fresh plums or prunes soaked overnight in tea (chopped)
1 teaspoon finely chopped rosemary
4oz/100g lard
1 egg (beaten)
1lb/450g lean lamb cut into cubes
Half teaspoon grated nutmeg
1oz/25g dripping
Half ounce/14g sugar

Set oven at 200C/400F/Gas Mark 6.

Fry the lamb in the dripping until browned, add the rosemary and nutmeg and leave over a low heat for a further 10 minutes.

Sift the flour and salt into a bowl and rub in the lard until the mixture is crumbly. Add sufficient cold water to make into a soft dough and leave to rest in a cool place for about 20 minutes. Lightly grease a deep pie plate and line with half the pastry rolled out. Place the apple slices on the base, sprinkle over the sugar, arrange the meat on the apples and cover with the chopped plums or prunes. Roll out the remaining pastry and cover the pie, sealing the edges well with the beaten egg. Do not stretch the pastry as it will shrink away from the edges during cooking. Make a couple of slits on the top to allow steam to escape and decorate with pastry trimmings. Brush over with egg and bake for 30-35 minutes or until golden brown and lamb and apples are quite tender. Serve with creamed potatoes and a green vegetable.

Recommended variety - Bramley/Newton Wonder

APPLE-GLAZED SPARE RIBS (for a Bar-b-que)

5lb/2¼kg spare ribs

Marinade -
1 onion (peeled and thinly sliced)
8fl.oz/225ml soy sauce
8fl.oz/225ml dry sherry
4 cloves of garlic (crushed)
2 tablespoons/30ml grated horseradish
1 tablespoon/15ml Dijon mustard
1 tablespoon peeled and grated fresh ginger root
1 tablespoon grated lemon rind
1 tablespoon/15ml fresh lemon juice
Dash of Tabasco

Glaze -
6 tablespoons/90ml apple juice
3oz/75g sugar
Dash grated nutmeg
Dash ground cloves
Half teaspoon cinnamon
One and a half teaspoons cornflour

Separate the spare ribs. To make the marinade - in a large bowl combine the onion, soy sauce, sherry, garlic, horseradish, mustard, ginger root, lemon rind and juice and Tabasco. Put all the spare ribs in the bowl and toss to cover well. Leave to marinate overnight, turning occasionally.

To make the glaze, mix the apple juice and all the other glaze ingredients in a small saucepan and bring to the boil. Heat for about 5 minutes until thickened. Set aside in a bowl.

Glaze the spare ribs and grill over a hot bar-b-que for about 45 minutes, basting them occasionally with the glaze. Serve immediately.

HAM WITH APPLE (serves 6)

6 large ham or gammon slices or steaks (about ½"/1cm thick)
5oz/150g soft light brown sugar
3oz/75g soft white breadcrumbs
6fl.oz/175ml pineapple juice

To garnish -
3 apples (peeled, cored and sliced into rings ¾"/2cm thick)
3oz/75g margarine

Remove rind from the ham or gammon and snip the fat at intervals to prevent it curling. Put slices in a large frying pan with a little water, heat to simmering point and simmer for 10 minutes, turning once. Drain. Lay the slices or steaks overlapping each other on a large, shallow ovenproof dish. Mix together the sugar and breadcrumbs, spread mixture over the meat and trickle the pineapple juice over them. Cook uncovered for 25 minutes.

While meat is cooking, melt the margarine in a frying pan and fry the apple rings until they are tender but not soft. Garnish the meat with the apple rings and serve immediately.

Recommended variety - Blenheim Orange/Newton Wonder

ROAST DUCK WITH APPLE SAUCE (suitable for diabetics)

1 x 3lb8oz/1.6kg duck
1lb8oz/675g potatoes
Salt & pepper
2oz/50g melted butter

Sauce -
8oz/225g chopped apple
4 tablespoons/60ml water
Knob of butter
Artificial sweetener to taste

Set oven at 180C/350F/Gas Mark 4.

Dry duck inside and out, rub skin with salt and prick all over with a fork. Place breast side down on a rack over a roasting tin and cook for 30 minutes. Remove from oven, turn duck over, prick all over again and return to oven for one hour. Meanwhile, parboil the potatoes for 5 minutes, drain and transfer to the roasting tin. Pour over the butter, sprinkle with salt and pepper and roast on top shelf for one hour.

To prepare the apple sauce, stew the apples in the water until pulpy, rub pulp through a sieve, return to pan and add the knob of butter and sweetener (if desired). Serve hot with the roast duck.

Recommended variety - Golden Noble/Dumelow's Seedling

PHEASANT WITH CREAM, CALVADOS AND APPLE

1 cooked roasting pheasant
Small glass Calvados/brandy/whisky (your own preference)
8oz/225g thick cream
2 sweet apples (peeled, cored and diced)

Carve pheasant while still hot and arrange slices in a heatproof serving dish.
Pour off the juices from the roasting into a small pan and let them bubble.
Pour in the warmed Calvados, brandy or whisky, set it alight, shake the pan and
when the flames have burnt out add the cream. Shake the pan again, lifting and
stirring the cream until it thickens. Season with a little salt and pepper. Pour
the sauce over the pheasant. Serve the meat with a side dish of the diced
apple which has been fried golden brown in butter and kept warm.

Recommended variety - Blenheim Orange

ROAST GOOSE WITH RUM-SOAKED APPLES

1 goose about 10lb/4.5kg
Salt and pepper
3 tablespoons cooking oil or dripping
1¹/₂pt/850ml poultry stock
4fl.oz/100ml dark rum

For the stuffing -
6 large eating apples (peeled, cored and soaked in rum for 4 hours)
3 finely chopped sage leaves or quarter teaspoon ground sage
Quarter teaspoon ground mace
12oz/350g fresh breadcrumbs

Set oven at 180C/350F/Gas Mark 4.

Remove giblets and wipe the goose clean inside and out. Mix the stuffing ingredients together and spoon into the body of the bird, any left over can be put in the neck cavity. Rub salt and pepper into the skin, prick goose all over and place on a rack over a roasting tin. Spread oil or dripping over the wings and legs. Cover the breast with a large piece of foil or greaseproof paper and place bird in the centre of a pre-heated oven.

Roast for 30 minutes, then spoon off excess fat and baste well with the warm poultry stock. Do this every 30 minutes. After two and a half hours remove the foil or greaseproof paper so the breast will become crisp and brown.

Place goose on a warm serving dish and keep warm. Strain off excess fat from pan juices and boil rapidly to reduce and use for gravy. Heat the rum in a ladle or small pan and pour over the bird, then set alight. Serve immediately.

Recommended variety - Bramley

ESCALOPE OF VEAL WITH CREAM, CALVADOS AND APPLE

2 escalopes of veal
Half a sweet apple (peeled, cored and cut into little cubes)
Quarter pint/150ml thick cream
1-2oz/25-50g butter
Juice of 1 lemon
Seasoning
2 tablespoons/30ml Calvados

Melt butter in a thick frying pan, when bubbling add the escalopes quickly and lightly brown each side. Add the apple cubes. Heat the Calvados in a little pan, set it alight and pour over the meat. At the same time, turn up the heat under the pan and shake pan until the flames die down. Pour in the cream and lower the heat. Cook gently for a further 2 minutes, stirring the sauce and mixing in the juices. When the cream has thickened, transfer to a heated serving dish, arranging the apple cubes on top of each escalope and pour sauce all round.

Recommended variety - Blenheim Orange/Charles Ross

TURKEY STUFFED WITH CHESTNUTS AND APPLES

12lb/5.5kg turkey
2lb/900g chestnuts
1lb/450g sweet apples (peeled, cored and sliced)
6oz/175g salted or fresh belly pork
Half pint/275ml milk
Quarter pint/150ml water
2 shallots (finely chopped)
Parsley (chopped)
1 egg (beaten)

Make an incision in the rounded part of the chestnut and roast for 10 to 15 minutes. Take out a few at a time and shell and skin them while still hot. Stew them in the milk and water until they are soft, about 30 minutes. Cut the pork into small cubes and cook for 10 minutes in a little water. Put apples in a saucepan and stew in a little water until reduced to a purée. Mix purée, cooked pork, roughly chopped chestnuts, salt, pepper, shallots and parsley and bind with the egg. Stuff the turkey with the mixture and rub the skin liberally with butter. If possible roast slowly on its side on a rack over a baking tray, covered with buttered paper or foil.

Set oven at 325F/170C/Gas Mark 3.

For a 12lb/5.5kg bird it will need about three and a half hours, turning over about half way through the cooking time. To make a sauce add a little white wine or sherry to the buttery juices from the pan and boil rapidly in a small pan.

Recommended variety - Bramley/Golden Noble

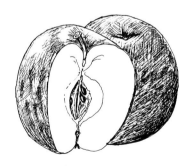

TWO TRIED AND TESTED RECIPES FOR STUFFING MIX -

APPLE & ONION STUFFING
Half a Bramley apple grated
Half an onion grated
Handful of seedless raisins
1 clove garlic crushed
8oz/225g of breadcrumbs
Salt & pepper
Teaspoon chopped parsley

Thoroughly mix all ingredients. Should make sufficient to stuff a 4-5lb
(1.8-2.2kg) chicken.

OLD SCOTTISH CHICKEN STUFFING
1lb good sausage meat
1 Bramley cooking apple (peeled, cored and grated)
1 medium sized onion (peeled and grated)
1 medium sized potato (peeled and grated)
1 standard egg (beaten)
Salt & pepper
3-4oz/75-100g medium oatmeal

Mix the grated apple, onion and potato with the sausage meat. Add the beaten
egg and season. Stir in enough oatmeal to make a sticky to dry consistency
mixture. Stuff your chicken.

PORK PIE WITH A DIFFERENCE (serves 4)

1lb8oz/675g cubed pork
1 large onion (peeled and sliced)
1 bay leaf
1 clove of garlic (crushed)
1 tablespoon tomato purée
1 tablespoon fresh chopped sage
Salt & black pepper
Half pint/275ml chicken stock
1lb/450g pears (peeled and thickly sliced)

Topping -
1lb/450g packet flaky pastry (thawed if frozen)
1 egg (beaten)

Set oven at 180C/350F/Gas Mark 4.

Put pork into a large casserole, add the onion, bay leaf, garlic, tomato purée, sage, seasoning and stock. Cook in the oven for 45 minutes and then transfer to a greased 2pt/1.1 litre pie dish, putting a funnel in centre of the dish. Arrange the pear slices on top of the meat mixture.

Increase oven heat to 200C/400F/Gas Mark 6. Roll out the pastry, lay a thin strip around the edge of the dish, dampen with water and lay remaining pastry on the top. Trim, flute the edges and decorate the top with spare pastry. Glaze top with the beaten egg and bake for 25-30 minutes or until top is golden brown.

NB. Apples can be used instead of pears in this recipe, but the pears do make a tasty and interesting alternative.

Recommended variety - Conference/Gorham

LOIN OF PORK WITH PEARS IN PERNOD

4 slices of boneless loin of pork
2oz/50g butter
Salt & pepper
Juice of 1 lemon
4 ripe dessert pears (peeled and quartered)
1 tablespoon of Pernod
4 tablespoons/60ml thick cream
Finely chopped fennel to garnish

Set oven at 190C/375F/Gas Mark 5.

Trim off any surplus fat from pork and sear both sides in one-third of the butter. Arrange the meat in a single layer in an oven dish, season with salt and pepper and sprinkle with half the lemon juice. Cook meat in the preheated oven for 15-20 minutes.

Slice the pears lengthways and sprinkle over the remaining lemon juice. Melt the rest of the butter in a pan and sauté the pears for 3-4 minutes or until soft, add the Pernod and cook for a further 1-2 minutes. Stir in the cream and meat juices from the pork.

Arrange the pears on top or beside the pork slices and spoon over the sauce. Garnish with the chopped fennel and serve immediately.

NB. The Pernod offsets the richness of the pork and sweetness of the pears.

Recommended variety - Comice/Conference/Concorde

PUDDINGS

APPLE PIE (serves 4)

8oz/225g apples (peeled, cored and sliced)
2oz/50g sugar
8oz/225g shortcrust pastry

Set oven at 220C/425F/Gas Mark 7.

Divide the pastry into two and roll out to fit an 8"/20cm greased pie plate. Line plate with pastry, fill with apple and cover, trim and seal edges well. Sprinkle with sugar. Make a slit in the top of the pie. Bake for 15 minutes on high heat and then for 30 minutes at 180C/350F/Gas Mark 4. When cooked dredge with sugar and serve hot or cold.

Recommended variety - Golden Noble/Dumelow's Seedling

OXFORDSHIRE APPLE PIE (serves 6-8)

12oz/350g cooking apples (peeled, cored and sliced)
2oz/50g sugar
1oz/25g currants
1/2oz/14g chopped candied peel
Pinch ground ginger and cinnamon
2fl.oz/50ml water
1lb puff pastry

Set oven at 220C/425F/Gas Mark 7.

Mix sliced apples thoroughly with the sugar, currants, peel and spices and arrange in a buttered pie dish. Add the water. Cover with the rolled out puff pastry and bake for 10-15 minutes on high heat and then for 30 minutes at 180C/350F/Gas Mark 4. Serve with custard or fresh cream.

Recommended variety - Bramley

GLOUCESTERSHIRE APPLE PIE (serves 8)

8oz/225g wholemeal flour
4oz/100g flour
6oz/175g butter
1lb8oz/675g prepared cooking apples (peeled, cored and chopped)
3oz/75g brown sugar
2oz/50g chopped walnuts
6oz/175g Double Gloucester cheese (cut into small cubes)
1 egg (lightly beaten)
Half teaspoon ground nutmeg

Set oven to 200C/400F/Gas Mark 6.

Mix the flours and rub in the butter until like fine breadcrumbs. Mix with sufficient cold water to form a soft dough and leave it to rest while preparing the filling. Put chopped apples in a pan with sugar and nutmeg and cook until soft. Roll out the pastry and line a deep greased pie dish. Arrange the cooked apple and cubed cheese evenly in the pastry case and sprinkle over the walnuts. Using the pastry trimmings, cut into strips, twist slightly and arrange over the filling forming a lattice pattern, pinching the joining edges. Brush with the egg and bake for about 35 minutes or until cooked and golden brown. Serve hot or cold with custard or ice cream.

Recommended variety - Annie Elizabeth

CRAB APPLE CAKE (serves 6)

12oz/350g crab apples (quartered, cored and chopped)
3 tablesoons/45ml honey
1 teaspoon ground cinnamon
8oz/225g wholewheat flour
Pinch sea salt
1 teaspoon bicarbonate of soda
4oz/100g butter
4oz/100g light brown sugar (Demerara)
Quarter pint/150ml natural yoghurt

Set oven to 200C/400F/Gas Mark 6.

Mix prepared apples in a bowl with the honey and half the cinnamon.
Put flour in a bowl with the salt, bicarb and the remaining cinnamon. Rub in the butter and lightly toss in the sugar. Make a well in the centre and pour in the yoghurt, mixing everything to a moist dough. Put the dough mixture into a buttered tin 2"/5cm deep and 8"x10"/20x25cm. Cover the top with the crab apples. Bake the cake for 30 minutes so the top browns and an inserted skewer comes out clean. Serve the cake hot with cream.

Recommended variety - Veitch's Scarlet

CRAB APPLE PUDDING (serves 4)

1lb/450g crab apples (washed and chopped)
Quarter pint/150ml water
2oz/50g light brown sugar
Pinch of ground cloves

Topping -
4oz/100g wheatmeal self raising flour
4oz/100g medium oatmeal
4oz/100g light brown sugar
Pinch ground cloves
4oz/100g butter
2 eggs (beaten)
4 tablespoons/60ml milk

Set oven at 180C/350F/Gas Mark 4.

Put apples in saucepan with water and set on a low heat. Cover and cook for about 25 minutes, stirring occasionally. Rub through a sieve to make a purée and stir in the sugar and ground cloves.

Make the topping while the apples are cooking. Mix flour, oatmeal, sugar and cloves together and make a well in the middle. Melt the butter and pour into the flour. Add the eggs and milk and beat with a wooden spoon until the mixture is smooth. Put the crab apple purée in a large, buttered ovenproof dish, cover with the pudding mixture and bake for 30 minutes until golden brown and firm. Serve hot with cream.

Recommended variety - Veitch's Scarlet

CRAB APPLE CRUMBLES (serves 4)

1lb/450g crab apples (washed, cored and chopped)
4oz/100g sultanas
One teaspoon ground cinnamon
4 tablespoons/60ml honey

Crumble mixture -
6oz/175g muesli base
4 tablespoons sesame seeds
4 tablespoons dessicated coconut
4 tablespoons/60ml sunflower oil

Set oven at 200C/400F/Gas Mark 6.

Put apples, sultanas, cinnamon and honey in bowl and mix well. Divide mixture between four small buttered ovenproof bowls. Mix together the muesli base, sesame seeds, coconut and oil and divide between bowls, covering apple mixture completely. Bake for 25 minutes until golden brown. Best eaten hot with cream or natural yoghurt.

Recommended variety - Veitch's Scarlet

FRENCH CREAM AND APPLE TART

1 x 10"/25cm shortcrust pastry shell prebaked

Custard cream -
6 tablespoons/3oz/75g sugar
Pinch of salt
3 tablespoons/2oz/50g cornflour
Quarter pint/150ml milk
Quarter pint/150ml single cream
3 egg yolks (lightly beaten)
1 tablespoon/15ml brandy or 1 teaspoon/5ml good vanilla essence
Quarter pint/150ml double or whipping cream

Apples -
1 tablespoon/15ml brandy
1 teaspoon/5ml lemon juice
4 large fragrant dessert apples (peeled, cored and thinly sliced)
2 tablespoons/30ml melted butter
1oz/25g caster sugar

To make the custard cream, mix the sugar, salt and cornflour together and blend in the milk and cream in a heavy based pan and bring the mixture to the boil, stirring and continue to simmer for 3-4 minutes. Remove the pan from the heat and cool the mixture slightly continuing to stir. Gradually beat in the egg yolks. Return the pan to a very low heat, continuing to stir constantly, for 3-4 minutes or until the custard is very thick and smooth. Do not allow mixture to bubble. Stir in the brandy or vanilla essence and leave to cool, beating occasionally to prevent a skin forming on the top. Put the custard aside in a covered bowl until you are ready to use it.

To prepare the apples, mix the brandy and lemon juice with 2 tablespoons /30ml cold water in a large bowl, add the prepared apples and turn them in the brandy mixture to coat them.

Whisk the double or whipping cream stiffly and fold it into the custard. Spread the custard cream over the base of the pastry shell, arrange the apple slices in overlapping concentric circles over the top, shaking off the excess moisture when taking them out of the bowl. Brush the apples with the melted butter and dust with caster sugar.

Place tart under a moderate grill and grill steadily for 15-20 minutes or until the surface is golden and lightly caramelized. If the pastry case starts to get too brown protect with a little crumpled foil.

Recommended variety - Blenheim Orange/Charles Ross

HONEY AND APPLE TART (serves 4-6)

12oz/350g cooking apples (peeled, cored and grated)
Half pint/150ml honey
Juice and rind of 1 lemon
6oz/175g fresh wholemeal breadcrumbs
9oz/250g short crust pastry

Set oven at 200C/400F/Gas Mark 6.

Mix grated apples with honey, lemon rind and juice and breadcrumbs. Roll out pastry on a lightly floured surface and use to line an 8"/20cm flan tin. Spoon in filling and level surface. Bake for 30-35 minutes until firm to the touch. Serve warm or cold.

Recommended variety - Bramley/Golden Noble

GERMAN APPLE PANCAKES

4 large apples (peeled, cored and sliced into thin rings)
4^{1}/$_{2}$oz/135g plain flour
1 teaspoon baking powder
Icing sugar
Salt
4 eggs (separated)
Half pint/275ml milk
Quarter pint/150ml double cream
1 teaspoon good vanilla essence
Butter

Sift the flour, baking powder, 1 tablespoon/15g icing sugar and salt into a bowl and mix. Make a well in the centre and work in the egg yolks, followed by the milk, cream and vanilla, beating vigorously to make a smooth batter.

To make the pancakes use an 8"-9"/20-23cm frying pan. Melt enough butter to swirl around the bottom of the pan and pour in a thin layer of batter to coat the entire surface. As the underside starts to cook, gently push in a few slices of the apple into the surface. Let the pancake brown on the underside and begin to turn firm on top. Slide pancake out carefully onto a large lightly greased plate and then return pancake to the pan to brown the other side. Serve apple-side up, dusted with icing sugar.

Recommended variety - well flavoured dessert or cooking apples - Newton Wonder/Blenheim Orange

CHINESE CARAMELIZED APPLES (serves 4)

4 sharp tasting cooking or eating apples (peeled, cored and quartered)
Lemon juice (optional)
Peanut oil for frying
Ice cubes
10oz/275g sugar
Sesame seeds

For the batter -
4 tablespoons/2oz/50g cornflour
3 tablespoons/1¹/₂oz/35g plain flour
4 egg whites

Cut quartered apples in half and to keep from discolouring toss in the lemon juice.

Using a wire whisk, mix the batter ingredients together to make a smooth, coating paste. Fold in the prepared apple and make sure each piece is thoroughly coated.

Pour enough oil into a wide, deep pan so that the cubes will float free of the bottom and deep-fry them in batches to a light golden colour, make sure the oil does not get too hot. Remove the fritters with a slotted spoon and drain on kitchen paper.

Just before serving, pour 8 tablespoons/120ml of the oil into another pan that will take a large batch of the fritters. Have ready a large bowl of iced water. Add the sugar to the oil and swirl the pan gently over a low heat until the sugar has melted and turned a light golden colour. As soon as the caramel is ready, drop in a batch of the fritters, turn them around with two forks so they are well coated and stick together in clusters. Lift the clusters out of the hot caramel and shake sesame seeds over them and drop them into the bowl of iced water. The syrup will instantly turn into a glassy caramel. Shake the chunks free of water and serve immediately.

Recommended variety - Cox/Charles Ross

CHERRY AND APPLE STRUDEL (serves 8)

2 cooking apples (peeled, cored and diced)
3oz/75g demerara sugar
1 teaspoon ground cinnamon
12oz/350g tinned or frozen red cherries (stoned)
2oz/50g sultanas
6 sheets filo pastry
2oz/50g butter (melted) + a little extra for greasing
1oz/25g icing sugar

Set oven at 180C/350F/Gas Mark 4.

Put apples in saucepan with two tablespoons of water and cover. Bring to boil and cook gently for 5 minutes until soft. Stir in the sugar, cinnamon, cherries and sultanas and remove from heat. Lay filo sheets out flat and brush each sheet with melted butter, carefully layering the sheets into a pile. Spread the apple mixture evenly over the pastry and then carefully roll up the pastry away from you. Lightly grease a baking tray, place the strudel on the sheet and bake for 35-40 minutes until golden. Remove from the oven and dust with icing sugar. Serve hot or cold in slices.

Recommended variety - Bramleys/Gloster

APPLE STRUDEL ICE CREAM

2oz/50g oats
2oz/50g chopped walnuts
12oz/350g cooking apple (peeled, cored and sliced)
Juice of half a lemon
2 tablespoons/30ml concentrated apple juice
Quarter pint/150ml natural yoghurt
1 teaspoon ground cinnamon
2 egg whites

Grind oats down to a flour in a grinder or liquidizer. Place walnuts, apple, lemon juice and apple juice in a saucepan, cover and cook over a low heat until puréed. Remove from heat and beat in the oat flour and cinnamon. Leave to cool and then fold in the yoghurt. Whisk the egg whites until stiff and fold into the mixture. Place in a shallow container and freeze. When nearly frozen break up with a fork and mash and return to freezer. Remove ice cream from freezer 25-30 minutes before serving to allow to soften to scoop out.

Recommended variety - Cox/Charles Ross

SPECIAL APPLE FRITTERS (serves 6)

For the batter -
5oz/150g plain flour
Salt
1 tablespoon/15ml liqueur (optional)
2 tablespoon/30ml oil
2 whites from large eggs

Apple mixture -
4 small apples (peeled, cored and sliced quarter inch/6mm thick rings)
Half teaspoon/2.5ml finely grated lemon rind
1 tablespoon/15ml lemon juice
1 tablespoon/15ml liqueur (optional)
2oz/50g icing sugar

Coating syrup -
1oz/25g sugar
6 tablespoons sieved apricot jam or thick dark orange marmalade

To finish -
4oz/100g sponge finger biscuits (very finely crushed)
Oil for deep-frying
Sifted icing sugar
Chilled, lightly whipped cream

To make the fritter batter sift the flour into a bowl with a pinch of salt. Make a well in the centre and gradually blend in quarter pint/150ml of lukewarm water, and the liqueur (if desired), followed by the oil. Beat vigorously to a thick, glossy cream, cover and set aside for at least 30 minutes.

Sprinkle the apple rings with lemon rind, the lemon juice mixed with the liqueur (if desired) and sifted icing sugar. Turn the slices to coat them evenly.

In a heavy pan, dissolve the sugar and jam over a low heat, diluting the mixture with enough water to make a syrup of coating consistency. Simmer the syrup for 1 minute and keep it warm. Coat each apple ring with the syrup, allowing the excess to drain off. Put the sponge finger crumbs on a large plate and as each apple ring is coated with the syrup, dip it into the crumbs. Pat them lightly but firmly on both sides and set aside.

Return to the batter mixture stirring in with a broad-bladed knife the egg whites and salt which have been beaten to form soft peaks.

Heat the oil for deep-frying to 190C/375F. Use two long skewers, one for coating the apple rings with batter and the other for taking them in and out of the oil. Deep-fry the apple rings until they are crisp and puffed, flipping them over once or twice. Drain on absorbent kitchen paper, dust with sifted icing sugar and serve immediately with cream.

Recommended variety - Charles Ross/Blenheim Orange

APPLE CHARLOTTE - (serves 4)

8oz/225g prepared (peeled, cored and sliced) Bramley apples
8oz/225g prepared (peeled, cored and sliced) Cox's eating apples
1oz/25g granulated sugar
1oz/25g brown sugar (preferably demerara)
5 slices bread with crusts removed
3oz/75g butter
1 egg

Set oven at 200C/400F/Gas Mark 6.

Cook apples with a little water and the sugar until soft. Allow to cool and beat with a fork, mixing in the egg yolk. Generously grease a one pint pudding basin and line bottom with baking parchment. Sprinkle the greased sides with the brown sugar. Melt the remaining butter in a pan, cut the bread into fingers and brush with the melted butter. Line the basin with the bread, overlapping to fill gaps, fill with the cold apple and make a lid of the buttered bread to fit snugly on top. Cover with an ovenproof plate with a weight. Stand basin in a baking tray (in case filling bubbles out) and bake for about 40 minutes. Remove plate and weight and return basin to oven for 10 minutes to brown the top. Leave to stand for about 5 minutes for turning out on to a heated plate and serve immediately with cream or custard.

APPLE MARMALADE CHARLOTTE

About 8oz/225g left-over bread and butter or plain bread
2oz/50g marmalade
Half pint/275ml milk
8oz/225g apples (peeled, cored and sliced)
1 egg
Sugar to taste

Set oven at 180C/350F/Gas Mark 4.

Put a layer of bread into a greased pie dish and cover with a layer of sliced apple and a little marmalade. Cover with the bread and add another layer of apple and ending with bread. Beat up the egg in the milk and pour over and bake for 30/35 minutes until golden brown. Serve hot.

Recommended variety - Blenheim Orange/Charlotte

APPLE CHARLOTTE A LA POLONAISE (serves 6)

Apple mixture -
3lb/1350g apples (peeled, cored and cut into small pieces)
Vanilla sugar (to taste)
2 teaspoons ground cinnamon
Finely grated rind of 1 orange (optional)
6oz/175g sultanas
Lemon juice
1 tablespoon/15ml butter

Pastry -
1lb/450g self-raising flour
1 teaspoon baking powder
5oz/150g butter (chilled)
2oz/50g pure lard or white vegetable fat (chilled)
2 eggs
4oz/100g caster sugar

Toss apples in vanilla sugar, cinnamon, orange rind (if used) and the sultanas. Sharpen the flavour if you wish with a few drops of lemon juice.

To make the pastry, sift the flour and baking powder into a bowl. Cut the butter and lard or vegetable fat into small pieces and rub into the flour until the mixture resembles breadcrumbs. Make a well in the centre. Beat the eggs and sugar together until fluffy and lemon coloured and work into the flour mixture by hand until they are blended into a dough. Knead briefly, roll into a ball and seal in plastic wrap or foil. Chill for at least 1 hour until very firm.

Set the oven at 200C/400F/Gas Mark 6.

Use a baking tin about 2"-3"/5-8cm deep and 10"/25cm by 12"/30cm, grease well and line the base and at least 2"/5cm up the side with two-thirds of the pastry, returning the remainder to the fridge to chill firm. Bake the pastry base for 30 minutes or until it is golden. Remove from the oven and allow to settle for a few minutes. Fill the case evenly with the apple mixture and dot the surface with the butter. Take the remaining chilled dough and grate it coarsely and evenly over the entire surface.

Return the charlotte to the oven and bake for 45 minutes to 1 hour or until it is a rich golden colour, the apples are soft and a piece of topping picked off the top tastes cooked.

Serve warm or cold, cut into rectangles, dusted with sifted icing sugar and accompanied with whipped cream.

Recommended variety - Blenheim Orange

SCANDINAVIAN APPLE CHARLOTTE (serves 4)

3oz/75g butter or margarine
8oz/225g fresh white breadcrumbs
2oz/50g demerara sugar
1lb8oz/675g cooking apples (peeled, cored and sliced)
1 lemon
2 tablespoons/30ml water
2oz/50g caster sugar
Quarter pint/150ml double cream
Coarsely grated chocolate

Melt butter in a frying pan, add the breadcrumbs and fry slowly, stirring frequently until very crisp and golden. When ready remove from heat and blend in the demerara sugar. Put apples in another pan with lemon juice, water and caster sugar, cover and cook until apples are soft and then mash to a purée. Leave to cool.

Put half the purée into a 2pint/1.1 litre serving dish and spread over half the breadcrumb mixture. Repeat with a layer of apple and then breadcrumbs. Allow to chill before serving then pipe or spread over the lightly whipped double cream and sprinkle over the grated chocolate.

Recommended variety - Blenheim Orange

APPLE CREAM (A quick and easy dessert with children in mind)

Peel, core and grate apples according to the quantity you need. Mix quickly with sweetened condensed milk and heap into glass dishes.

Recommended variety - Cox

APPLE CREAM SPONGE

2lb/900g apples (peeled, cored and sliced)
Sponge cake or any stale pieces of plain cake
2 eggs
1pt/575ml milk

Cook apples with a little water until they resemble apple sauce and leave to cool. Sweeten a little and pour half of the apples over the sponge pieces arranged in a dish. Make a little custard with the egg yolks and milk. Whisk the egg whites and mix into the remaining apples until mixture is creamy. Put custard on top of sponge cake and apples and then top with the creamy mixture.

Recommended variety - Cox/Charles Ross

APPLE DELIGHT

6oz/175g self-raising flour
3oz/75g lard
1lb/450g cooking apples (peeled, cored and sliced)
2oz/50g sugar
1 egg white
A pinch of salt

Set oven at 190C/375F/Gas Mark 5.

Make a short pastry by rubbing the fat, salt and flour together and adding water. Roll out pastry and line a sandwich tin and bake until golden brown.

Cook apples with the sugar in a little water until very soft and then beat until soft. Pour into the pastry case. Whisk the egg white until stiff and spread evenly on the apple. Return to the oven for a few minutes to brown and when cold decorate with a little blackcurrant jam. Serve cold with custard.

Recommended variety - Newton Wonder/Golden Noble

APPLE MERINGUE FLAN

1 baked 7"/18cm pastry case
1lb/450g cooking apples (peeled, cored and finely sliced)
Half ounce/14g butter
Sugar to taste
Rind of half a lemon
1 egg yolk

For meringue:
2 egg whites
4oz/100g caster sugar

Set oven at 150C/300F/Gas Mark 2.

Cook apples in butter until quite soft and then sieve or liquidize. Add lemon rind, egg yolk and sugar to taste. Whisk egg whites stiffly, then whisk in 2oz/50g of the sugar until shiny. Fold in the remaining 2oz/50g of sugar. Spread base of the flan case with raspberry jam, orange marmalade or apricot jam, put apple on top and spread over meringue, ensuring it reaches the pastry edges. Sift over a little caster sugar and place in oven for about 20 minutes to set.

Recommended variety - Bramley

APPLE SNOW (serves 4)

1½lb/675g cooking apples (peeled, cored and cut into quarters)
Juice of 1 lemon
4oz/100g caster sugar
2 large eggs
4 tablespoons/60ml water

Put apples and lemon juice into a pan with the water and cook very gently to a soft pulp. Leave to cool and strain off any juice. Beat the sugar into the apple pulp until smooth. Separate the eggs, beat the whites until stiff and beat into the apple purée. Pile the mixture into dishes and decorate. Serve with cream.

Recommended variety - Early Victoria/Keswick Codlin

SPICED APPLE TURNOVERS

8oz/225g cooking apples (peeled, cored and chopped)
1oz/25g brown sugar
1 tablespoon/15ml brandy or rum
1oz/25g sultanas or raisins
Half ounce/14g chopped dates
1 dessertspoon/10g marmalade
Grated rind of half a lemon
Half teaspoon mixed spice
8oz/225g puff pastry
Beaten egg to glaze

Set oven at 200C/400F/Gas Mark 6.

Put apple, sugar and brandy or rum into a saucepan and cook gently to a pulp. Leave to cool and add the other filling ingredients. Roll out the pastry thinly and cut circles approximately 5"/13cm in diameter using a saucer or bowl as a guide. Place a little of the apple mixture in the centre of each pastry circle, dampen the edges with water and bring top edge of circle to the bottom to form the 'turnover'. Seal well, put on a greased baking tray, brush with the beaten egg and bake for 20 minutes.

Leave to cool and dredge with icing sugar.

Recommended variety - Newton Wonder/Annie Elizabeth

APPLE AND SYRUP TART WITH OATMEAL PASTRY

For the pastry -
4oz/100g flour
2oz/50g fat
4oz/100g fine oatmeal
Pinch of salt
Water to mix

For the filling -
1lb/450g apples (peeled, cored and sliced)
Few cloves
3 tablespoons/45ml golden syrup
2oz/50g sultanas
2oz/50g sugar
2 tablespoons brown breadcrumbs

Set oven at 180C/350F/Gas Mark 4.

To make the pastry mix the flour, oatmeal and salt together and rub in the fat.
Form a stiff paste with a little water, then roll out and line a greased deep
round tin with the pastry.

Stew apples with the cloves in a little water until tender and strain off any
liquid. Stir in the sugar and pour mixture into pastry case, sprinkling the
breadcrumbs over the top. Cover with warmed golden syrup add the sultanas.
Bake in a moderate oven for 30 minutes. Can be served hot or cold.

Recommended variety - Bramley

APPLE TANSY

3 large soft apples (peeled, cored and sliced)
Sugar to taste
1pt/575ml milk
3 eggs
A little mixed spice
1 cupful/225g fine breadcrumbs

Set oven at 150C/300F/Gas Mark 2.

Cook apples until soft and pour into a greased fireproof dish. Beat the eggs,
add them to the milk, sweeten to taste and add a pinch of mixed spice and
nutmeg. Pour this mixture over the breadcrumbs and beat lightly and then pour
the mixture over the apples. Bake very slowly until set.

Recommended variety - Bramley/Golden Noble

STUFFED APPLES WITH BLACKBERRIES

One apple per person (peeled and cored)
Blackberries
Sugar to taste

Set oven at 180C/350F/Gas Mark 4.

Place apples in a greased ovenproof dish. Press blackberries to a pulp and mix with sugar or golden syrup. Put blackberry mixture in centre of apples and any left over put around apples with a little water. Bake until soft. Serve hot.

Recommended variety - Peasgood Nonsuch

SPICED APPLE CAKE

For the pastry -
3oz/75g flour
3oz/75g cornflour
2oz/50g butter
2oz/50g caster sugar
Half teaspoon mixed spice
1 egg yolk
Pinch of salt

For the filling -
1lb/450g apples (peeled, cored and sliced)
3oz/75g sugar
Rind of half a lemon
A little water
Teacupful of cake or biscuit crumbs

Set oven at 170C/325F/Gas Mark 3.

Put apples in a saucepan with the sugar, lemon rind and a little water and stew until the apples are pulpy. Turn out to cool. Make the pastry by mixing all the dry ingredients together, rubbing in the butter and binding with the egg yolk and a little water. Do not make pastry too soft. Knead pastry until smooth and roll out thinly. Grease a dish and line with the just over half of the pastry and sprinkle half the breadcrumbs at the bottom. Fill up with the apple mixture and cover with the rest of the breadcrumbs. Roll out the remaining pastry and cover dish, dampening edges and sealing in the usual way. Bake for about 1 hour, remove from oven and sprinkle with sugar.

Recommended variety - Lord Derby/Annie Elizabeth

CHOCOLATE APPLE STIRABOUT

4oz/100g flour
2oz/50g sugar
1 tablespoon cocoa
2oz/50g margarine
3 or 4 cooking apples (peeled, cored and chopped)
Pinch of salt
Milk to mix

Set oven at 220C/425F/Gas Mark 7.

Mix flour, cocoa and salt and rub in margarine. Add the sugar and apples and mix with the milk to make a thick batter. Pour into a greased baking dish and bake for 20-30 minutes. Serve hot with golden syrup.

Recommended variety - Golden Noble

APPLE CRUNCHIE

1lb/450g cooking apples (peeled, cored and cut up)
Lemon juice
2oz/50g margarine
4oz/100g soft brown sugar
Quick porridge oats

Set oven at 180C/350F/Gas Mark 4.

Put apples in a greased pie dish and sprinkle with lemon juice. Mix together the margarine, sugar and enough oats to make a firm mixture. Spread over the apples and bake for about 20 minutes. Serve hot with cream.

Recommended variety - Lord Derby/Newton Wonder

KENTISH HONEYED FRUIT SALAD

4oz/100g red cherries (stoned)
4oz/100g raspberries (hulled)
4oz/100g strawberries (hulled)
4oz/100g William pears (peeled and sliced)
4oz/100g dessert apples (peeled and sliced)
2 tablespoons lemon juice
2 tablespoons Kentish honey
1pt/575ml water

Sprinkle the apples with half the lemon juice to prevent browning. Heat the water and honey together to make a syrup and add the sliced apples and pears. Poach very gently over a low heat to soften and leave to cool. Add the raspberries, strawberries and cherries and a tablespoon of the lemon juice and stir. Put in a bowl and serve with pouring cream.

Recommended variety - Discovery/Cox

APPLE SHAPE (serves 4)

1lb/450g cooking apples (peeled, cored and chopped)
2oz/50g sugar
Half ounce/14g gelatine
Rind and juice of 1 lemon
Cochineal
Half pint/275ml water

Stew apples with the sugar, lemon rind and juice and water. When quite soft rub through a sieve. Melt the gelatine in a little water and add to the apple pulp. Mix well and add the cochineal, sufficient to colour to a pale pink. Turn mixture into a wet mould and leave to set.

Recommended variety - Annie Elizabeth

DUCHESS APPLES (serves 4-6)

6 small apples (peeled and cored)
6 rounds of bread and butter
2 tablespoons apricot jam
1oz/25g sweet almonds (blanched and cut into strips)
2oz/50g granulated sugar

Put apples in a pan with the sugar and enough boiling water to cover and simmer until soft but not broken. Brown slices of bread and butter in a quick oven or frying pan. Strain apples, leaving the syrup in the pan and reduce by boiling rapidly until there is only about quarter of a pint/150ml. Add the apricot jam and stir until hot. Put an apple on each piece of bread, cover with the apricot syrup and stick in the almonds. If the apricot syrup is too sweet for your taste add the juice of half a lemon.

Recommended variety - Cox

PRUNE AND APPLE JELLY

1lb/450g cooking apples (peeled, cored and chopped)
4oz/100g prunes (soaked overnight)
3oz/75g sugar
Strip of lemon peel
Half ounce/14g gelatine

Put prunes and apples in pan. Add the sugar and lemon peel and cook until the prunes are quite soft. Rub through sieve and return mixture to the pan. Dissolve the gelatine in a little water and add to the mixture. Stir gently over a low heat until thoroughly blended. Turn into a wet mould and leave to set. Serve with custard or cream, flavoured with lemon.

Recommended variety - Most varieties

POTATO APPLE CAKE

1lb8oz/675g cooked potatoes
1 teaspoon salt
3 medium-sized apples (peeled, cored and sliced)
5oz/125g flour
1¹/₂oz/35g melted margarine

Set oven at 180C/350F/Gas Mark 4.

Mash potatoes carefully while they are still hot with a little of the margarine. Place on a board and sprinkle with salt. Add the melted margarine and knead in enough flour to make a soft, pliable dough. (Take care not to add too much flour). Roll out and divide into two cakes. Place the sliced apples on one round and place the other cake on top, pinching the edges together. Place on a greased dish and bake for about 30 minutes. When cooked, split the cake open, turn the top over and put small pieces of margarine on with some of the sugar. Put the top back and return to the oven until the margarine and sugar are melted.

Recommended variety - Newton Wonder

NORFOLK PUDDING

8oz/225g apples (peeled, cored and sliced)
4oz/100g flour
1 egg
Half pint/275ml milk
1oz/25g dripping
Quarter teaspoon salt

Set oven at 220C/425F/Gas Mark 7.

Put flour and salt in a basin, add the egg and beat to a smooth batter with the milk. Heat the dripping in a pie dish, put in the apples and pour the batter over. Bake for 30 minutes and serve immediately.

Recommended variety - Lord Derby/Blenheim Orange

TOFFEE APPLES

1lb/450g sugar
1¹/₂oz/40g butter
Half pint/250ml water
1 teaspoon/5ml vinegar
2 level tablespoon/30ml golden syrup
6 small sweet apples
6 toffee apple sticks

Put all sugar, butter, water, vinegar and golden syrup into a heavy based saucepan and stir over a steady heat, until sugar has dissolved.

While the ingredients are coming slowly to the boil, polish the apples and insert a stick, pointed end first through each apple. Bring the ingredients to a 'rolling' boil and cook until the mixture reaches 'hard-crack' stage. Quickly roll each apple round in the toffee mix and place on an oiled tin to set.

Recommended variety - Cox/Spartan/Gala

APPLE AMBER

1lb8oz/675g cooking apples (thinly peeled, cored and sliced)
2oz/50g granulated sugar
Rind and juice of half a lemon
1oz/25g butter
2 egg yolks

Meringue -
2 egg whites
Small pinch of salt
4oz/100g caster sugar

Set oven at 170C/325F/Gas Mark 3.

Put apples, granulated sugar, juice and lemon rind into a saucepan, cover and cook gently to a pulp, stirring occasionally. Crush with a potato masher or beat well with a wooden spoon. Beat in butter a small piece at a time while the purée is hot and follow with the egg yolks. Pour mixture into a 6"/18cm pie dish. Whisk egg whites with salt until stiff in a bowl, add 2 teaspoons of the measured sugar and beat for half a minute. Fold in remaining sugar with a metal spoon and pile on top of apple. Dust with caster sugar and bake for about 30 minutes until top is crisp and golden brown.

Recommended variety - Golden Noble

APPLE DUMPLINGS

4 medium size cooking apples (peeled and cored)
2oz/50g sugar
A few cloves
Shortcrust pastry

Set oven at 220C/425F/Gas Mark 7.

Divide pastry into 4 and roll out sufficient to cover one apple each. Place the whole apples on the pastry and fill the centres with sugar. Cover the apples with the pastry, sealing the edges well. Put on a greased tin and bake for 30 minutes.

Recommended variety - Newton Wonder/Bramley

APPLE AND ORANGE FLAN

For pastry -
4oz/100g plain flour
2oz/50g caster sugar
2 egg yolks
2oz/50g butter
2-3 drops vanilla essence

For filling -
2lb/900g cooking apples (peeled, cored, quartered and sliced)
2-3oz/50-75g granulated sugar
Grated rind of 2 oranges

To finish -
2 seedless oranges (remove peel and pith and sliced into rounds)
4 tablespoons/60ml apricot glaze

To prepare pastry make a well in the flour and put in sugar, egg yolks, butter and vanilla. Using the fingertips of one hand only, work all these added ingredients to a paste. Draw in the flour quickly and knead until smooth. Chill pastry for at least 30 minutes in refrigerator.

Set oven at 190C/375F/Gas Mark 5. Roll out pastry, line flan ring and bake blind in pre-heated oven for 15 minutes.

To prepare filling, put apples in a buttered pan, cover with lid and cook to a pulp. Rub through a sieve and return purée to pan with sugar and orange rind. Cook until thick, stirring all the time. Turn out and leave to cool a little. Fill the flan case with the purée and smooth top and arrange sliced oranges on the top. Make the glaze by dissolving the jam in a little water and lemon juice, sieve and then boil until clear. Brush the oranges with the warm glaze. Leave to set and serve cold.

Recommended variety - Lord Derby/Bramley

APPLE AND ORANGE PUDDING

12oz/350g cooking apples (peeled, cored and sliced)
3oz/75g butter
Sugar to sweeten
6oz/175g stale cake crumbs
Rind and juice of 1 orange

Set oven at 190C/375F/Gas Mark 5.

Melt 1oz/25g of the butter in a pan, add the apple and cook until soft but not pulpy. Remove from heat and add sugar to taste. Melt remaining butter in another pan, stir in the crumbs, half of the orange rind and all the orange juice. Grease a 7"/18cm sandwich tin and spread half the crumb mixture over the base. Cover with the apple to within half an inch/1cm of the sides and cover with the rest of the crumbs. Bake for 15 minutes. Invert on to a warmed plate and leave in tin for 5 minutes. Lift off tin and sprinkle over rest of orange rind. Serve with custard or cream.

Recommended variety - Bramley

BAKED APPLE PUDDING

1lb8oz/675g apples (peeled, cored and sliced)
2 tablespoons/30ml water
1oz/25g margarine
2oz/50g sugar
2oz/50g breadcrumbs
2 eggs

Set oven at 220C/425F/Gas Mark 7.

Stew apples gently in water and when cooked mash them with a fork. Add the margarine and the sugar and then the eggs and half the breadcrumbs. Place in a greased cake tin and sprinkle the remainder of the crumbs on top. Cover with greased paper and bake for 1 hour. Turn out on to a hot dish and serve with custard.

Recommended variety - Golden Noble/Annie Elizabeth

BAKED APPLE GINGER PUDDING

1lb/450g cooking apples (peeled, cored and sliced)
4oz/100g flour
1 teaspoon baking powder
Half teaspoon ground ginger
4oz/100g golden syrup
1oz/25g margarine
1 egg
2oz/50g sugar

Set oven at 200C/400F/Gas Mark 6.

Stew apples with a tablespoon of water and the sugar. When cooked mash with a fork and place in a greased pie dish. Warm the syrup and margarine, add the beaten egg and pour all on to the flour, baking powder and ginger. Beat well together and place on top of apples. Sprinkle with blanched almonds if liked and bake for about 30 minutes.

Recommended variety - Bramley

FLAMING APPLE TART

For the pastry -
6oz/175g flour
3oz/75g butter
Pinch of salt
A little water

For the filling -
1lb8oz/675g apples (peeled, cored and sliced)
4oz/100g brown sugar
Half teaspoon cinnamon
2oz/50g butter
Half glass water
Rum

Set oven at 220C/425F/Gas Mark 7.

To make pastry mix together flour, sugar and salt. Cut the butter into small lumps and mix into flour and sugar using fingertips. Roll out and line a 7"/18cm tin and bake blind.

Fry sliced apples gently in butter, add the sugar, cinnamon and half glass of water and a little rum. Cover and allow to cook gently until apples are soft. Arrange slices on base of baked flan, sprinkle with brown sugar and "flambee" it. Serve either warm or cold.

Recommended variety - Bramley

APPLE BONFIRE

8-10 even size dessert apples (washed and cored)
Grated rind and juice of 1 lemon
8oz/225g mincemeat
1-2 tablespoons/15-30ml sherry or cider
Quarter pint/150ml water
2oz/50g granulated sugar
5-7 sugar lumps
2-3 tablespoons/30-45ml brandy or sherry

Set oven at 180C/350F/Gas Mark 4.

Put apples in a deep casserole dish with lid. Mix the rind and lemon juice with the mincemeat and moisten with a little sherry or cider and fill the centre of the apples with this mixture. Boil the water and sugar together to make a light syrup and pour round the apples. Cover apples with buttered paper and lid of casserole and cook for 20-25 minutes or until tender. Baste during cooking.

Allow apples to cool a little and then pile them up in a shallow ovenproof dish. Soak the sugar lumps in brandy or sherry and dot them around the apples. Reduce any syrup left and pour round.

To serve - set fire to the soaked sugar lumps and serve immediately.
(Note: Brandy will give a better lasting flame than sherry).

Recommended variety - Cox

WEST COUNTRY PUDDING

2oz/50g butter
4oz/100g soft brown sugar
8oz/225g suet crust pastry
2lb/900g apples (peeled, cored and sliced)
2 tablespoons/30ml water
Juice and rind of 2 lemons

Set oven at 200C/400F/Gas Mark 6.

Cream butter, sugar and lemon juice together and put in the bottom of a greased pudding basin. Roll out suet crust and line basin over top of mixture and up sides, leaving enough to make a top. Fill with apples, lemon rind and water and put suet crust on top, sealing well. Cook on high heat until brown and then turn down to 170C/325F/Gas Mark 3 - about 2 hours altogether. Turn out on to heated dish large enough for the sauce which has cooked at the bottom of the basin.

Recommended variety - Bramley/Newton Wonder

APPLE & PLUM PUDDING

8oz/225g self-raising flour
4oz/100g finely shredded suet
1 teaspoon baking powder
Pinch of salt
1lb/450g plums or damsons (cut in half and stones removed)
8oz/225g cooking apples (peeled, cored and thinly sliced)
6oz/175g white sugar
1 tablespoon/25g stale sponge cake crumbs

Mix flour, baking powder, salt and suet in a bowl and make a soft dough with cold water. Knead lightly on a floured board until pliable and roll out, reserving one-third for top. Line a greased 2pint/1.1 litre pudding basin with pastry, trimming the edge, and layer in the basin the fruit and sugar with cake crumbs in between. Add one tablespoon/15ml water. Roll out remaining pastry to fit top, dampen edges and cover fruit, sealing edges well. Cover with buttered greaseproof paper and then white pudding cloth and steam or boil for 2¹/₂ - 3 hours (be sure to keep water topped up with boiling water). Serve from basin with pouring custard or cream.

Recommended variety - Lord Derby/Early Victoria

OLD FASHIONED APPLE DESSERT

4 large cooking apples (cored and roughly chopped)
3 tablespoons/45ml white wine
3oz/75g soft brown sugar
Pinch of powdered cinnamon
1 heaped tablespoon/25g crumbled stale cake crumbs
1oz/25g butter
1 egg yolk

Put unpeeled apples in pan with white wine and stir over low heat until apples are soft. Mash apples through a sieve and add the sugar while the purée is still hot. Allow to cool slightly and then add the cinnamon and cake crumbs. Later flake in the butter and lightly forked egg yolk. Turn into a well greased mould and press down firmly. Chill thoroughly and turn out on to serving dish and decorate, if desired.

Recommended variety - Newton Wonder/Charles Ross

FLAMING APPLES

4 large juicy and crisp dessert apples (washed, cored and peeled)
2oz/50g raisins
2oz/50g candied peel
4oz/100g chopped hazelnuts or almonds
Pinch of grated nutmeg
2fl.oz/50ml water
1oz/25g butter
1oz/25g caster sugar
4 tablespoons/60ml brandy

Set oven at 200C/400F/Gas Mark 6.

Place apples in a greased ovenproof dish. Mix raisins, peel, nuts, spice and sugar in a small bowl and then stuff the centres of the apples with the mixture, pressing down firmly. Score round the skin of the apples about one third of the way down. Put and water and butter in the dish and cook on centre shelf for about one and a half hours, basting apples with buttery water about every half hour until tender. Remove from the oven and carefully take off top rim of skin above the incision. Warm the brandy, pour over each apple, ignite at the point of serving and bring to the table flaming. Serve with whipped cream.

Recommended variety - Cox/Ribston Pippin/Worcester Pearmain

ADAM AND EVE PUDDING (serves 6)

1lb/450g cooking apples (peeled, cored and sliced)
6oz/175g caster sugar
1 tablespoon/15ml lemon juice
4oz/100g butter
2 eggs (beaten)
1 teaspoon grated lemon rind
4oz/100g self-raising flour
Pinch of salt

Set oven at 180C/350F/Gas Mark 4.

Arrange the apples in a deep buttered pie dish, sprinkling each layer with the lemon juice and half the sugar. Cream together the butter and rest of the sugar, add the eggs and flour alternately and beat until mixture is light and fluffy, add the lemon rind last. Spoon the mixture over the apples, stand dish on baking sheet and cook for about one and a quarter hours until the sponge is risen and golden brown. Remove from oven and dredge with icing sugar, if desired. Other serving ideas - whipped cream with a tablespoon of sherry, or pinch of ginger or rosewater added.

Recommended variety - Lord Derby/Golden Noble

VILLAGE APPLE CAKE

6oz/175g self-raising flour
4oz/100g butter
1lb/450g tart apples (peeled, cored and sliced)
3oz/75g caster sugar
1 egg
3oz/75g granulated sugar

Set oven at 180C/350F/Gas Mark 4.

Stew apples with a little water until soft, add the granulated sugar and leave to cool. Cream the butter and caster sugar together until light and fluffy, beat in the egg and flour until it is quite stiff. Cut in half, roll out one piece and line a well-greased sandwich tin. Fill with the cold apple, roll out remaining cake dough and fit on top, sealing edges well. Bake in a pre-heated oven for about one hour when it should be golden brown and firm to touch. Leave to cool in tin and serve dredged with granulated sugar.

Recommended variety - Bramley

COTSWOLD APPLE DUMPLING (serves 4)

8oz/225g self-raising flour
4oz/100g shredded suet
Pinch of salt
1/4 pint/150ml cold water
4 cooking apples (peeled and cored)
4 cloves
4 dessertspoons sugar
About half ounce/14g butter

Make a suet crust by mixing the flour, salt and suet together and sufficient cold water to form a smooth, pliable dough. Cut into four pieces. Roll out each piece lightly on a floured board. Stand an apple on the centre of each piece of pastry, fill the centre with the sugar (well pressed down), and put a sliver of butter on top with a clove. Brush the edges of the pastry with water, gather it round the apple, bring to the top and pinch together to seal it completely. Tie each dumpling in a well-floured pudding cloth and lower into a pan of boiling water. Keep boiling for 45-50 minutes, replenishing with boiling water as required. Serve hot with custard.

Recommended variety - Newton Wonder/Bramley

BAKED APPLE DUMPLINGS WITH PLUM SAUCE (serves 4)

4 large dessert apples (peeled and cored)
1lb/450g puff pastry
4oz/100g white marzipan (cut into 4 pieces)
1 egg (lightly beaten)
1lb/450g red plums (stoned)
2oz/50g granulated sugar
1 tablespoon/15ml lemon juice
Mint leaves to garnish
Two drops of almond essence

Set oven at 190C/375F/Gas Mark 5.

Cut pastry into 4 squares and roll out each piece on a floured board large enough to encase apples. Stand apples in centre of each pastry square and roll each piece of marzipan into a plug to fit the centre of each apple. Brush the edges of the pastry with the egg, draw pastry up to the top and pinch edges to seal. Place each dumpling seal side down on a greased baking sheet. With pastry trimmings cut small leaf shapes and arrange on top of each dumpling, brushing with egg to seal and then completely glaze with remaining egg. Chill for 15 minutes before baking in a pre-heated oven for about 40 minutes or until the pastry is puffed and golden brown and apples are tender (pierce with a skewer to test).

Make the sauce by stewing the plums with the sugar in a very small amount of water until they are very soft. Purée or liquidise until smooth, add the lemon juice to taste and the drops of almond essence. Spoon the sauce on the individual plates and place the baked apple in the centre. Best served hot.

Recommended variety - Cox/Worcester Pearmain

APPLE CRUMBLE (serves 4)

1lb.8oz/675g cooking apples (wiped, cored and sliced)
3 tablespoons/45ml water
4oz/100g raw brown sugar
1 teaspoon mixed spice
3oz/75g butter or margarine
6oz/175g flour (white or wholemeal)

Set oven at 200C/400F/Gas Mark 6.

Place apples, water, mixed spice and half the sugar in a saucepan and simmer gently for about 10 minutes - do not allow apples to become 'mashy'. Put apples in a 2pt/1.1litre lightly greased ovenproof dish and leave to cool. Rub butter into flour until the mixture resembles breadcrumbs and stir in the remaining sugar. Press crumble topping onto the apples and bake for 20-25 minutes. Serve warm.

Recommended variety - Lord Derby/Bramley

APPLE CRUMBLE - with a difference (serves 6)

3oz/75g wholemeal flour
2oz/50g rolled oats
1 tablespoon sunflower seeds
1 tablespoon dessicated coconut
3oz/75g soft margarine
Half teaspoon cinnamon
1oz/25g demerara sugar
1lb8oz/675g cooking apples (peeled, cored and thinly sliced)
Juice of 1 lemon (sprinkled over sliced apples)
Few cloves

Set oven at 200C/400F/Gas Mark 6.

Mix flour, oats and seeds, rub in the margarine and stir in the cinnamon and sugar. Place apples and lemon juice in saucepan and cook gently for two minutes with a few tablespoons of water. Turn into a deep lightly oiled dish and add the cloves. Cover with the crumble topping and bake for 20-25 minutes. Serve hot or cold with cream or natural yoghurt.

Recommended variety - Bramley

BLACKBERRY AND APPLE CRUMBLE (serves 4)

1lb/450g cooking apples (cored and sliced)
1 lemon
8oz/225g blackberries
2oz/50g wholemeal flour
2oz/50g rolled oats
3oz/75g soft margarine
2oz/50g finely chopped dates
1oz/25g sunflower seeds

Set oven at 200C/400F/Gas Mark 6.

Place apples in saucepan and sprinkle over lemon juice to prevent browning.
Wash blackberries, add to the apples and cook covered over a low heat for 5
minutes. Turn fruit into a deep lightly oiled dish. Mix flour and oats together,
rub in margarine and stir in the dates and sunflower seeds. Put mixture on top
of fruit and bake for 25 minutes. Serve hot with cream or plain yoghurt.

Recommended variety - Bramley/Lord Derby

APPLE AND ORANGE CRUMBLE (serves 4-6)

1lb 8oz/675g cooking apples (peeled, cored and sliced)
Grated rind and juice of 1 orange
1oz/25g light soft brown sugar
4oz/100g plain flour
2oz/50g plain wholemeal flour
3oz/75g butter
1¹/₂oz/40g icing sugar (sieved)
Quarter teaspoon ground cinnamon

Set oven at 200C/400F/Gas Mark 6.

Put apples, orange rind, juice and brown sugar in a large ovenproof serving dish.
Put the flours in a mixing bowl and rub in the butter until mixture resembles
fine breadcrumbs. Stir in the icing sugar and cinnamon. Sprinkle the crumble
topping over the apple and bake for 30-40 minutes until crisp and golden.
Serve hot with fresh cream or custard.

For a change substitute 3oz/75g of the flour with rolled oats, bran flakes or
oatmeal. Cinnamon can be replaced with mixed spice or ginger.

Recommended variety - Newton Wonder/Dumelow's Seedling

DUTCH APPLE CAKE (serves 6)

6oz/175g wholemeal flour
2oz/50g oat flour
1 teaspoon baking powder
5oz/150g unsalted butter or soft margarine
2 eggs (separated)
1 lemon
2lb/900g cooking apples (washed, cored and sliced)
18 dried apricots (soaked overnight)
4oz/100g raisins
1 teaspoon cinnamon
2oz/50g ground almonds

Set oven at 180C/350F/Gas Mark 4.

Lightly grease a 9"/23cm cake tin. To make pastry sieve flour and baking powder into bowl and rub in fat until mixture resembles breadcrumbs. Lightly beat the egg yolks and add to the pastry with a tablespoon of lemon juice. Bind to make a soft dough, roll out on a floured board, leaving sufficient for a lid, and line the tin. Roll out remainder for the lid. Cook unpeeled sliced apples over a low heat for five minutes with a few tablespoons of water and stir to ensure even cooking; then drain. In another pan boil the apricots for five minutes with a little water and drain. Fill the prepared pastry case with layers of apple, apricots and raisins, mix the spice and ground almonds together and sprinkle on top. Brush edge of pie with egg white and place pastry lid in position. Glaze and bake for 45-50 minutes.

Recommended variety - Bramley

APPLE TART (serves 4)

4oz/100g wholemeal flour
2oz/50g oat flour
2oz/50g soft margarine
4 small Cox's apples (washed, cored and sliced) or 1lb/450g
of other fruit, i.e. plums
2 tablespoons clear honey

Topping -
1oz/25g soft margarine
1 tablespoon clear honey
2oz/50g oats

Set oven at 190C/375F/Gas Mark 5.

Lightly oil an 8"/20cm flan ring or dish. Sieve flours into mixing bowl and rub in fat until mixture resembles breadcrumbs. Bind to make a soft dough with a little cold water. Roll out on floured surface and line flan ring or dish. Weight pastry down and bake blind for 10 minutes. Blanch apples for two minutes in boiling water and drain. Arrange the sliced apples on the pastry case and brush with clear honey.

To make topping, melt the margarine and honey in a pan, remove from heat and stir in the oats. Sprinkle around the edges of the flan ring or dish and bake for 20 minutes.

Recommended variety - Cox

NOTTINGHAM APPLE PUDDING (serves 6)

6 even-sized cooking apples (peeled and cored)
3oz/75g butter
3oz/75g caster sugar
Nutmeg
Cinnamon
3oz/75g flour
Water
3 eggs (well beaten)
Salt
Milk

Set oven at 200C/400F/Gas Mark 6.

Cream butter and sugar and add pinch of nutmeg and cinnamon. Fill the centre of each apple with the mixture and place in a well buttered ovenproof dish. Blend flour with a little cold water and add the eggs with a pinch of salt and sufficient milk to make a thick creamy batter. Pour over the apples and bake for 50 minutes.

Recommended variety - Bramley

APPLE TRIFLE (serves 2)

2 small buns or pieces of plain cake
2 teaspoons of raspberry jam
1 orange
8oz/225g cooking apples (peeled, cored and very thinly sliced)
Half ounce/14g butter
Squeeze of lemon juice
1-2 teaspoons sugar

4 tablespoons/60ml double cream

Cut across buns, sandwich together with jam and place in small dish or two
sundae glasses. Grate rind finely from orange and cover to stop it discolouring.
Squeeze juice from orange and pour over cake. Melt butter in small pan, add
the lemon juice and apples and cook over low heat until soft but not pulpy.
Sweeten to taste. Spread apple mixture over cake and leave until cold. Whip
cream, cover apples and decorate with orange rind.

Recommended variety - Keswick Codlin/Golden Noble

NORMANDY APPLE TART

1lb8oz/675g hard sweet apples (peeled and cored)
1¹/₂oz/30g butter
3oz/75g white sugar

For crumbly pastry -
6oz/175g plain flour
3oz/75g butter
Pinch of salt
3 teaspoons white sugar
2-4 tablespoons/30-60ml ice cold water

Set oven at 200C/400F/Gas Mark 6.

Melt butter and put in sliced apples and sugar and cook gently until apples are
golden and transparent. Turn slices over carefully being sure not to break them
or shake pan gently if closely packed. Leave to cool. To make the pastry rub the
butter into the flour, salt and sugar. Moisten gradually with water but the less
water used the lighter the pastry will be. Shape pastry into a ball and spread it
lightly with your hands into a buttered 8"/20cm flan tin. Brush the edges with
thin cream or milk. Arrange the sliced apples in overlapping circles keeping a
well-shaped slice for the centre. Bake with tin on a baking sheet in a preheated
oven for 30-35 minutes. Remove from oven and pour over the buttery juices
with a sprinkling of sugar and return to oven for one minute. Best served hot
but pastry should not soften when cold.

Recommended variety - Worcester Pearmain

APPLE MOUSSE AND HAZELNUT TART (serves 6)

1lb/450g hazelnuts
3oz/100g butter
4oz/100g honey
1 teaspoon ground cinnamon
10oz/275g muesli base

For the filling -
1lb/450g cooking apples (peeled, cored and chopped)
3 tablespoons/45ml honey
6 tablespoons/90ml dry cider or water
1 teaspoon ground cinnamon
Half ounce/14g gelatin
2 eggs (separated)
Quarter pint/150ml thick cream

Set oven at 170C/325F/Gas Mark 3.

Shell hazelnuts and toast in a moderate oven for 10 minutes, leave to cool and then rub off skins. Keep back 13 nuts and grind the rest in a blender or coffee grinder. Put the butter in a saucepan with the honey and cinnamon and melt on a low heat. Stir in the ground nuts and muesli base until it has absorbed the butter mixture. Well grease a 10"/25cm flan tin and press the muesli mixture over the base and sides in an even layer. Put in refrigerator to set.

Put apples in a saucepan with honey and 4 tablespoons/60ml of the cider. Add the cinnamon, cover and leave on low heat for 15 minutes. Remove from heat and rub through sieve. Soak gelatin in the remaining cider. Return the apple purée to the saucepan on a low heat, beat in the egg yolks and stir, without boiling, until mixture will coat the back of a wooden spoon. Melt the gelatin in a small pan and stir into the apple mixture. Remove from heat and leave to cool until almost setting. Meanwhile, whip the cream and egg whites separately. Fold half the cream into the apples and then all the egg whites. Pour the mousse mixture into the flan case and chill for about an hour before serving. Use remaining whipped cream to decorate, put a small portion in the centre and twelve more round the edge and top each one with a hazelnut.

Recommended variety - Bramley

APPLE NUT TART (serves 6)

9oz/250g plain flour
5oz/150g caster sugar
4¹/₂oz/135g butter (cut into pieces)
1 egg
1lb/450g dessert apples (peeled, cored and sliced)
2oz/50g hazelnuts (coarsely ground)
1 teaspoon ground cinnamon
Juice of 1 lemon
3 tablespoons/45ml apricot brandy (optional)
4oz/100g apricot jam
2oz/50g chopped hazelnuts

Set oven at 220C/425F/Gas Mark 7.

Sieve flour and 4oz/100g of sugar and rub in butter until mixture resembles breadcrumbs. Make a well in the centre, add the egg and mix, using a knife, when mixture becomes firmer, use fingers. Knead mixture until it becomes a smooth dough, then wrap in greasepoof paper and chill for at least 30 minutes. Roll out pastry and line a greased 8"/20cm pie dish. Layer the sliced apples and ground hazelnuts in pastry case, sprinkle over the cinnamon, remaining sugar, lemon juice and apricot brandy (if using). Put the apricot jam in a small saucepan, heat gently until melted and then pour over layered apples and hazelnut. Sprinkle top with chopped hazelnuts. Bake in preheated oven for 35-40 minutes or until fruit is soft and tart is golden brown.

Recommended variety - Cox/Worcester Pearmain/Spartan

DAMSON AND APPLE COBBLER (serves 6)

For the top -
6oz/175g wholewheat flour
2 teaspoons caraway seeds
Half teaspoon ground cinnamon
Half teaspoon baking powder
3oz/75g lard
2oz/50g demerara sugar
2 eggs (beaten)

Filling -
8oz/225g damsons (halved and stoned)
12oz/350g cooking apples (peeled, cored and sliced)
Pinch ground cloves
5oz/150g demerara sugar

Set oven at 180C/350F/Gas Mark 4.

Mix flour, caraway seeds, cinnamon and baking powder in a bowl and rub in the lard as for pastry. Toss in the sugar. Make a well in the centre and mix in the eggs using a wooden spoon to beat the mixture smooth. Put damsons and apples in a bowl and mix in the cloves and sugar. Put fruit mixture in a greased ovenproof 10"/25cm flan dish and spread the cobbler mixture evenly on the top. Bake for 35 minutes until golden brown. Serve hot with cream or natural yoghurt.

Recommended variety - Early Victoria/Lord Derby

DATE AND APPLE SQUARES (serves 4-6)

1lb/450g cooking apples (peeled, cored and diced)
2oz/50g shelled walnuts (chopped)
4oz/100g stoned dates (chopped)
4oz/100g self-raising flour (white or wholemeal can be used)
4oz/100g raw brown sugar
1 tablespoon/15ml clear honey
1oz/25g butter (melted)
1 egg
Pinch of salt

Set oven at 200C/400F/Gas Mark 6.

Place all ingredients in a large bowl and mix well to combine evenly. Spread mixture in a lightly greased 8"/20cm square shallow tin and bake for about half an hour or until golden and risen. Cut into squares and serve warm with fresh cream.

Recommended variety - Newton Wonder

DEVON APPLE CAKE (serves 6)

8oz/225g wholemeal self raising flour
Quarter teaspoon salt
1 teaspoon ground cinnamon
1 teaspoon mixed spice
4oz/100g raw brown sugar
4oz/100g butter or margarine
12oz/350g cooking apples (washed, cored and roughly chopped)
1 egg (beaten)

Set oven at 190C/375F/Gas Mark 5.

Grease and line the base of a 7½"/19cm square cake tin. Put flour, salt, cinnamon, mixed spice and sugar in a basin and rub in the butter or margarine until mixture resembles fine crumbs. Add the apples and beaten egg to the mixture and stir quickly to combine. Spread evenly in the tin and bake for about half an hour, until risen and firm to the touch. Leave to cool in the tin before cutting into squares.

Recommended variety - Lord Derby/Bramley

APPLE SWIRL (serves 4)

1lb/450g cooking apples (peeled, cored and chopped)
1oz/25g butter or margarine
2oz/50g raw brown sugar
Pinch of ground cloves
Grated rind of half a lemon
Half pint/275ml natural yoghurt

Place all the ingredients, except the yoghurt, in a pan and cook over gentle heat, stirring occasionally, until apples are 'pulpy'. Stir briskly to give a 'rough' purée and leave to cool. In a glass serving dish or individual dishes, spoon alternate spoonfuls of yoghurt and apple until it is all used up. Using a knife, swirl mixtures to make a decorative effect. Serve chilled.

Recommended variety - Bramley

APPLE CHUNKY DESSERT (serves 4)

2 small dessert apples (wiped, cored and finely chopped)
Quarter pint/150ml soured cream
2 tablespoons/30ml milk
1oz/25g chopped walnuts
2 tablespoons/30ml thin honey
3 tablespoons bran
8 apples slices (to decorate)

Mix the soured cream and milk in a basin and stir in the remaining ingredients.
Transfer to individual serving dishes and decorate with sliced apple. Can be kept
in a refrigerator for several days but it will tend to thicken. Can be thinned down
by adding a little milk.

Recommended variety - Cox/Worcester Pearmain

GENOESE APPLE CAKE (serves 6)

4 eggs
5oz/150g caster sugar
5oz/150g plain flour
1 teaspoon baking powder
Pinch of salt
4oz/100g butter (melted and cooled)
6 tablespoons/90ml milk
Finely grated rind of 1 lemon
1lb8oz/675g apples (peeled, cored and thinly sliced)
1-2 tablespoons/5-10ml vegetable oil
1-2 tablespoons dried breadcrumbs
Icing sugar to finish

Set oven at 180C/350F/Gas Mark 4.

Put eggs and sugar in a heatproof bowl standing over a pan of gently simmering water.
Whisk for 10-15 minutes until the mixture is thick and pale. Remove bowl from heat and
continue whisking until the mixture is cool. Sift the flour with the baking powder and salt
and fold half of this mixture gently into the whisked eggs and sugar. Slowly trickle the
melted butter round the edge and fold it into the mixture gently. Fold in the remaining
flour and then the milk and lemon rind. Fold in the apples. Brush inside of a 9"/23cm
cake tin with oil, sprinkle with breadcrumbs (shaking off excess) and pour in the cake
mixture. Bake for about 40 minutes, testing with a skewer inserted into the centre.
Remove from oven and leave in tin for about 5 minutes and then turn out onto a wire
rack. Sift icing sugar over cake just before serving.

Recommended variety - Golden Delicious

APPLE SPONGE CAKE

5oz/150g caster sugar
5oz/150g plain flour
5oz/150g melted cooled butter
6 eggs (whites and yolks separated)
Zest of 1 lemon
1lb/450g apples (peeled, cored and sliced not too thinly)

Set oven at 180C/350F/Gas Mark 4.

To make a light sponge - sift flour two or three times. Whisk egg whites to form stiff peaks, beat in half the sugar and gently fold in the rest using using a large metal spoon. Lightly fork the egg yolks in a separate bowl and fold them and the lemon zest into the egg whites. Then carefully fold in the sifted flour and melted butter. Pour just under half the mixture into a greased, floured and sugared 10"/26cm spring form or savarin mould. Place in a pre-heated oven for about 10 minutes to set the mixture. Remove from oven and gently lay the sliced apple over set mixture. Cover with the remaining sponge mixture, return to the oven and bake for a further 45 minutes or until it is well browned and shrunk away from the side of the tin (test with a skewer if felt necessary) and bear in mind that more fruit used will lengthen the cooking time.

Recommended variety - Bramley/Cox

BAKED APPLE AND COCONUT PUDDING (serves 6)

Finely grated rind and juice of 1 lemon
5oz/150g soft light brown sugar
6 medium eating apples, each weighing about 4oz/100g (peeled, cored and sliced)
4oz/100g butter
2 eggs (separated)
4oz/100g plain wholemeal flour
1½ teaspoons baking powder
1oz/25g dessicated coconut
4 tablespoons apricot jam (warmed)
Toasted shredded coconut (to decorate)

Set oven at 170C/325F/Gas Mark 3.

Pour lemon juice into bowl and stir in the 2 tablespoons/25g of sugar. Add the apples ensuring they are well coated. In a separate bowl gradually beat remaining 4oz/100g sugar into the butter until well blended, add the lemon rind and then beat in the egg yolks, one at a time. Stir in the flour, baking powder and dessicated coconut. Whisk the egg whites until stiff and then fold into the creamed mixture. Spoon into a lightly greased 10"/25cm fluted flan dish and press the apples into the mixture, spooning over any remaining juices. Stand dish on a baking sheet and cook for 1-1¼ hours or until well browned and firm to touch, covering lightly with greaseproof paper if necessary. Cool for about 15 minutes, then brush with the apricot jam and scatter over the toasted shredded coconut. Serve warm with custard.

Recommended variety - Cox

APPLE AND HAZELNUT LAYER (serves 8)

3oz/75g hazelnuts (shelled)
3oz/75g butter
2oz/50g caster sugar
5oz/150g plain flour
Pinch of salt
1lb/450g Cox's apples (peeled, cored and sliced)
1 tablespoon apricot jam or marmalade
Grated rind of 1 lemon
1 tablespoon candied peel (chopped)
2 tablespoons currants
2 tablespoons sultanas
Icing sugar, whipped fresh cream and hazelnuts, to decorate

Set oven at 190C/375F/Gas Mark 5.

Cut out two 8"/20cm circles of greaseproof paper. Reserve 8 nuts and finely
chop the remainder. Cream the butter and sugar until pale and fluffy, stir in
the flour, salt and chopped nuts and form into a ball. Chill for 30 minutes. Put
apple in a saucepan with the jam and lemon rind and cook over a low heat for
5 minutes, until soft. Add the candied peel and dried fruit and simmer for a
further 5 minutes. Divide the pastry in half, place on the sheets of greaseproof
paper and roll into two circles. Transfer to greased baking sheets. Bake for
7-10 minutes until light brown. Cut one circle into 8 triangles while warm and
leave to cool. Just before serving, place the complete circle on a serving plate
and cover with the apple mixture. Arrange triangles on the top, dust with icing
sugar, pipe cream on top and decorate apple layer with hazelnuts.

Recommended variety - Cox

WEST COUNTRY APPLE CAKE

4oz/100g butter
6oz/175g dark soft brown sugar
2 eggs (beaten)
8oz/225g plain wholemeal flour
1 teaspoon ground mixed spice
1 teaspoon ground cinnamon
2 teaspoon baking powder
1lb/450g cooking apples (peeled, cored and chopped)
3-4 tablespoons/45-60ml fresh milk
1 tablespoon/15ml clear honey
1 tablespoon light demerara sugar

Set oven at 170C/325F/Gas Mark 3.

Grease and line a deep 7"/18cm round cake tin with greaseproof paper. Cream the butter
and sugar together until pale and fluffy, add the eggs (a little at a time) beating well
after each addition. Add the flour, spices and baking powder and mix well. Fold in the
apples and enough milk to make a soft dropping consistency. Put mixture into tin and
bake for one and half hours until well risen and firm to the touch. Turn out to cool on a
wire rack. When cold brush with honey and sprinkle over the demerara sugar to decorate.
Can be served warm as a pudding and is best consumed within two days.

Recommended variety - Golden Noble/Blenheim Orange

APPLE BAKESTONE CAKE

8oz/225g shortcrust pastry
12oz/350g cooking apples (peeled, cored and finely sliced)
Half ounce/14g butter
2oz/50g soft brown sugar
Quarter teaspoon nutmeg

Put butter in a saucepan, add the apples, sugar and nutmeg and cover. Stew gently,
stirring frequently to prevent sticking for about 10 minutes. The apples should still be
fairly firm. Divide the pastry into two and roll out each piece into a round about
7"/18cm across. Moisten the rim of one round, spread the apple on top to within half
an inch/1.5cm of the edge and place the other round on top, pressing the edges lightly
together. Brush a griddle or heavy frying pan with oil before heating. To test the heat,
sprinkle a little flour on the surface and when it turns golden brown the heat is right.
Using a fish slice lift the cake onto the griddle or frying pan and cook for 10 minutes
until golden brown. Turn it over very carefully and cook the other side for 10 minutes.
Dredge with sugar and serve immediately with cream or custard.

Recommended variety - Lord Derby/Newton Wonder

APPLE CRISPS

4 good-sized cooking apples (peeled, cored and sliced)
Half cup/125ml margarine
1 cup/225ml brown sugar (Use same size cup for measuring)
1 cup/225ml flour

Set oven on 220C/425F/Gas Mark 7.

Grease a baking dish and three-quarters fill with the sliced apple. Work the margarine, sugar and flour together until mixture is like granulated sugar and spread it over the apples. Bake for 10 minutes and then reduce the heat to 180C/350F/Gas Mark 4 and cook until apples are soft and the mixture browned. Serve with cream or a thin custard.

Recommended variety - Blenheim Orange/Newton Wonder

APPLE AND SULTANA CREME BRULEE (serves 6)

1lb/450g dessert apples (peeled, cored and chopped)
2 tablespoons/30ml lemon juice
1oz/25g sultanas
1 pint/575ml double cream
1 cinnamon stick
3 egg yolks
2oz/50g caster sugar
2oz/50g demerara sugar

Put apples, lemon juice and 4 tablespoons/60ml water in a pan, cover and simmer over a gentle heat, stirring, for 15-20 minutes until the apples are pulpy. Stir in the sultanas and set aside. Bring three quarters of a pint/425ml of the cream to the boil with the cinnamon stick. Cover and set the mixture aside for 10 minutes, then remove the cinnamon. Whisk together the egg yolks and caster sugar until pale, then whisk in the remaining quarter pint/150ml cream. Stir this into the heated cream and cook, stirring over a moderate heat for 15 minutes until the mixture has thickened in the pan. Divide the apple mixture equally between 6 ramekin dishes, topping with the cream mixture. Leave to cool and then chill. Sprinkle each dish with demerara sugar and place under a fierce grill for 2-3 minutes or until the sugar has melted and bubbles. Leave to cool and then chill for 1 hour before serving.

Recommended variety - Cox/Charles Ross

APPLE AND BLACKBERRY CREAM (serves 4-6)

1lb/450g apples (peeled, cored and sliced)
8oz/225g blackberries
2oz/50g caster sugar
Half pint/275ml milk
Quarter pint/150ml cream (lightly whipped)
Half ounce/14g gelatine

Cook fruit with a little water until soft and then press through sieve. Add the sugar and mix well. Soak the gelatine in a 5fl.oz/150ml cold water, then stir over a gentle heat until dissolved. Strain it into the fruit pulp. Bring milk to just below boiling point and stir in the fruit mixture. Add the cream and stir over a very gentle heat until quite hot and well mixed. Turn into a wet mould.

Recommended variety - Bramley/Lord Derby

APPLE AND BLACKBERRY WHIP (serves 4)

1lb/450g cooking apples (peeled, cored and chopped)
8oz/225g soft blackberries
4oz/100g granulated sugar
2oz/50g caster sugar
2 egg whites

Press blackberries through a fine sieve to extract the juice. Put juice in a saucepan and add the apples and granulated sugar. Cook until tender and then rub through a sieve and set aside until cold. Whisk the egg whites and stir in the caster sugar. Beat the fruit pulp for a few minutes, add the whipped egg whites and continue beating until stiff. Pile into glass dishes.

Recommended variety - Early Victoria/Lord Derby/Bramley

APPLES WITH PINEAPPLE (serves 4)

1 small tin sliced pineapple
4 large cooking apples (peeled and cored)
2oz/50g pudding rice
1oz/25g granulated sugar
Half pint/250ml milk
1 egg yolk
Rind of 1 lemon
Butter or margarine

For the syrup -
2oz/50g sugar
Quarter pint/150ml water
Half a lemon
Quarter pint/150ml pineapple juice
1 teaspoon arrowroot or cornflour

Set the oven at 170C/325F/Gas Mark 3.

Put the rice, milk and a small piece of lemon rind in a saucepan and simmer very gently until the mixture is thick and soft. Remove from heat and stir in the beaten egg yolk and a dessertspoon of sugar. Continue to stir over a gentle heat for a few more minutes and then spread it in a dish and leave to get cold.

To make the syrup put the sugar and water in a saucepan with the strained juice of half a lemon and the pineapple juice and boil for ten minutes. Mix the arrowroot or cornflour with a little water and add it to the juice. Continue to stir while the syrup boils for a further 5 minutes. Strain and cool before using.

Fill the centres of the apples with the sugar and butter, put them in a baking dish with two tablespoons/30ml of water and bake until soft, basting frequently with the juice. Leave until cold.

Cut the rice into four rounds and arrange them in a glass dish, put a slice of pineapple on each and top with the baked apples, filling the centres with finely chopped pineapple and pouring the syrup gently over them.

Recommended variety - Bramley

APPLE CUSTARD

1lb8oz/675g cooking apples (peeled, cored and chopped)
6oz/175g fresh breadcrumbs
2oz/50g butter
2 eggs
Half pint/275ml milk
Pinch of cinnamon
6oz/175g granulated sugar
A little caster sugar

Set oven at 180C/350F/Gas Mark 4.

Generously butter a pie dish and sprinkle over a layer of breadcrumbs. Put in half the apples with half the granulated sugar, add a layer of breadcrumbs and then the remaining apples and sugar, finishing with a light layer of breadcrumbs. Beat the eggs well and mix with the milk and cinnamon and pour over layers. Bake for 45 - 60 minutes. Remove from oven and sprinkle over caster sugar. Serve hot.

Recommended variety - Lord Derby

APPLE SLICE

8oz/225g plain flour (sifted with a pinch of salt)
3oz/75g white cooking fat
Squeeze of lemon juice
Quarter pint/150ml iced water
3oz/75g butter
1lb/450g cooking apples (peeled, cored and sliced)
1oz/25g candied peel (finely chopped)
2oz/50g sultanas
Half teaspoon cinnamon

For the glaze -
1 egg white or 1 beaten egg
Caster sugar
Half ounce/14g blanched and halved almonds
2 tablespoons apricot glaze (apricot jam warmed with a little water)

Set oven at 220C/425F/Gas Mark 7.

Rub half the cooking fat into the sifted flour. Add the lemon juice to the iced water and use to mix with the flour to a soft dough. Roll out dough to an oblong three times as long as wide, and using half the butter, place small pats over two thirds of the dough. Fold in three, placing the plain third against dough with fat. Seal the edges lightly and leave to chill. Give pastry a quarter turn, roll out again and repeat the process using the remaining cooking fat and butter. Chill well. Roll and fold once more and chill again.

Prepare the filling by mixing the apple, candied peel, sultanas and cinnamon together.

Roll out pastry to an oblong about 14"x10" (35x25cms) and divide into unequal portions, ie. 14"x4" and 14"x6" (35x10cm and 35x15cm). Place the smaller piece on a baking tray and leaving a 1"/25mm clear edge of pastry put the filling down the centre, piling it up well. Fold the other portion of pastry in half lengthways and with a sharp knife make cuts through both layers at right angles to the fold and at 1"/25mm intervals and not quite to the "open" edge. Dampen the edges of the smaller piece of pastry, open up the slit piece, place it over the fruit filling with the cuts gaping slightly and seal the edges well.
Chill slice for 10 minutes.

Glaze the slice with egg white or beaten egg, scatter over the almonds and sprinkle with caster sugar. Bake for 20 minutes at 220C/425F/Gas Mark 7, then reduce the heat to 190C/375F/Gas Mark 5 for 10-15 minutes until golden and crisp. Remove from oven and place on a cooling rack and brush lightly with the apricot glaze.

Recommended variety - Bramley

105

MERINGUE APPLES WITH CHOCOLATE SAUCE

6 large dessert apples (peeled and cored)
2oz/50g sugar (dissolved in 15fl.oz/425ml water)
1 vanilla pod or 3-4 drops vanilla essence

Stuffing mixture -
4oz/100g dried fruit
Small piece candied peel
Half ounce/14g butter

Meringue -
2 egg whites
4oz/100g caster sugar

Chocolate sauce -
2 tablespoons cocoa
1 tablespoon sugar

Set oven at 140C/275F/Gas Mark 1.

Bring sugar syrup to the boil and boil steadily for 10 minutes, flavour with the vanilla. Poach apples carefully in the syrup ensuring they are tender right through. Remove from pan with draining spoon, reserving syrup and arrange in an ovenproof dish.

To prepare the stuffing, chop the fruit and candied peel and put in a pan with the butter and 1 tablespoon of the apple syrup. Stir over a gentle heat for 5 minutes and then stuff the mixture in the centre of the apples. To prepare the meringue, whip the egg whites until stiff and then whisk in 1 tablespoon of the sugar for 1 minute and, using a tablespoon, fold in the remainder carefully. Cover each apple with the meringue using a spoon or piped, dust with caster sugar and bake for 15-20 minutes until golden brown.

While the apples are cooking make the chocolate sauce. Mix the cocoa and sugar to a paste with a little of the poaching syrup, add the mixture to the remaining syrup in a pan and simmer gently for 15 minutes. Pour hot sauce round apples before serving.

Recommended variety - Cox/Blenheim Orange

UPSIDE-DOWN APPLE TART

1lb/450g apples (peeled, cored and thinly sliced)
2oz/50g butter
2oz/50g granulated sugar
8oz/225g puff pastry

Set oven at 180C/350F/Gas Mark 4.

Put the butter, apples and sugar in a round ovenproof dish and cook in oven for about 30 minutes until the apples are lightly cooked. Remove dish from oven and turn up heat to 220C/425F/Gas Mark 7. Roll out pastry and cover the dish, sealing the edges well. Return to oven for about 15 minutes until well cooked and golden brown. Take out and turn upside-down on a warmed dish and serve immediately with whipped cream.

Recommended variety - Blenheim Orange

CARAMELIZED UPSIDE-DOWN APPLE TART

Sweet pastry -
8oz/225g wholemeal flour
Pinch mixed spice
4oz/100g butter
1oz/25g raw cane sugar (powdered in a grinder)
1 tablespoon/15ml vegetable oil
1 egg (beaten)

Topping -
6oz/175g raw cane sugar
1oz/25g butter
2fl.oz/50ml water
1lb/450g apples (peeled, cored, quartered and thinly and evenly sliced)

Mix flour and spices in a bowl and rub in the butter. Stir in the sugar, oil and beaten egg to make a firm batter. Roll in a ball and put in refrigerator for 30 minutes.

Make the caramel by cooking the sugar, butter and water in pan and pour into a heatproof glass flan dish, spreading it out to cover the entire dish. Arrange the sliced apples on the caramel so they overlap slightly making an attractive pattern.

Set the oven at 200C/400F/Gas Mark 6.

Roll out the pastry (about 5mm thick) to fit the dish and lay over the apples. Bake for 35-40 minutes. Remove from oven, allow to cool for 6 minutes and then run a knife round the dish to loosen the tart, turning upside-down onto a warmed dish. Serve immediately.

Recommended variety - Cox/Golden Delicious

APPLE CHARTREUSE

1 large cooking apple (wiped, remove eye and stalk and sliced)
Half pint/275ml water
8oz/225g granulated sugar
Rind and juice of 1 lemon
2lb/900g apples (peeled, cored and thinly sliced)
4oz/100g candied fruit (mixture of glace cherries, angelica, pineapple, apricot
and orange peel all chopped)

Put sliced cooking apple in saucepan with water, cover and simmer gently until
pulpy. Pour into strainer over a bowl and leave until all the juice has dripped
through. Measure out 7½fl.oz/215ml and put in a large shallow pan with the
sugar, rind and lemon juice and set on a low heat. When the sugar has dissolved
boil steadily for 5 minutes, take off heat and remove lemon rind.

Put the dessert apples into the syrup, cover the pan and cook gently for 10-12
minutes. At this point turn the apples only once or twice taking care not to
break slices or allow the syrup to boil - it should simmer gently. Take the lid off
the pan and continue cooking until there is just enough syrup to moisten the
apples. Take off the heat, add the candied fruits, cover the pan and leave until
the apples look clear. Tip mixture into a wet cake tin or soufflé dish and leave in
a cool place the set. (The pectin in the apples will be sufficient to set the
mixture).

Turn out the chartreuse onto a dish and serve with fresh cream, a soured
cream sauce or a sharp rum and apricot sauce.

Recommended varieties - Cox/Orange Pippin/Egremont/Russet/Sturmer Pippin

APPLE LAYER PUDDING

Suet Pastry -
12oz/350g self-raising flour
Pinch of salt
5oz/150g shredded suet
Cold water to mix

Filling -
1lb/450g apples (peeled, cored and thinly sliced)
6oz/175g raisins
3oz/75g brown sugar

Grease a 2pint/1.1 litre pudding basin. Put the flour and salt in a bowl, stir in the suet and mix to a soft, but not sticky dough. Cut pastry in half and roll one piece into a circle, sufficient to line the basin. Press firmly to the sides and overlap edge of basin.

Mix the apples, raisins and brown sugar and spoon half the mixture into the basin. Roll a third of the remaining pastry sufficient to cover mixture and pack remaining mixture into top half. Roll out remaining pastry and cover top, moistening edges to ensure the edges are sealed.

Cover the pudding with a double layer of greased greaseproof paper or a floured oven cloth, leaving room for pudding to expand (pleat top of paper or cloth) and tie firmly with string. Steam pudding for two hours, checking frequently for water level and topping up with boiling water as necessary. Turn out on warmed dish and serve immediately.

Recommended variety - Bramley

SUNDAY APPLE LAYER PUDDING (serves 6)

1 packet trifle sponge cakes
1lb/450g apples (peeled, cored and sliced)
4oz/100g mincemeat
2oz/50g butter
3 tablespoons/45ml sieved apricot jam

Set oven at 180C/350F/Gas Mark 4.

Well butter a 1 1/2pt/850ml ovenproof dish and spread the remaining butter over the trifle sponges. Arrange half of the sponges in the dish, cutting to fit. Top the sponges with half the sliced apples and spread over half the mincemeat. Cover with another layer of sponge, mincemeat and apples, arranging final layer neatly. Cover surface with apricot jam. Bake for about 45 minutes. Serve hot with custard or cream.

Recommended variety - Bramley

CHOCOLATE APPLE LAYER PUDDING

1lb/450g apples (cooked, puréed and sweetened to taste)
8oz/225g packet milk chocolate digestive biscuits
1 dessert apple (washed, quartered and sliced and tossed in lemon juice)
A little lemon juice
1 glace cherry

Set oven at 200C/400F/Gas Mark 6.

Crush biscuits to fine crumbs in a polythene bag. Into a 1½pt/850ml ovenproof dish put half the apple purée and sprinkle over half the biscuit crumbs. Spread over the rest of the apple and top with the remaining crumbs. Bake for about 25 minutes until the top is golden brown and remove from oven. Arrange the slices of dessert apple in the centre of the pudding to form petals and place cherry in the middle. Serve pudding slightly warm with custard or cream.

Recommended variety - Bramley

APPLE CHEESE CRISP (serves 6-8)

1lb2oz/500g sliced apples
2fl.oz/50ml water
Juice and rind of 1 lemon
4oz/100g granulated sugar
Half teaspoon ground nutmeg
Half teaspoon ground cinnamon

For the topping -
3oz/75g self raising flour
Pinch salt
2oz/50g butter or margarine
3oz/75g brown sugar
3oz/75g grated cheddar cheese

Set oven at 170C/325F/Gas Mark 3.

Mix apples, water, lemon juice and rind and spread in a lightly greased pie dish. Stir spices into sugar and sprinkle over apples.

To prepare the topping rub the butter or margarine into the flour and salt, add the brown sugar and then lightly work in the cheese. Spread topping over the apples and bake for about 35 minutes or until the apples are tender and the top is golden brown. Serve hot or cold with whipped cream.

Recommended variety - Bramley

BAKED APPLE TAPIOCA (serves 6-8)

1lb2oz/500g sliced apples
2fl oz/50ml hot water
Juice and rind of 1 lemon
1¹/₂oz/35g tapioca
4oz/100g brown sugar
3oz/75g granulated sugar
Half teaspoon ground nutmeg
Half teaspoon ground cinnamon
Pinch salt
Knob of butter or margarine

Set the oven at 180C/350F/Gas Mark 4.

Mix the sliced apples, hot water, lemon juice and rind in a lightly greased deep dish and bake for about 15 minutes. Remove from the oven. Mix the tapioca, sugars, salt and spices and add to the apples. Put a knob or two of butter or margarine on the top and return dish to the oven to bake until the apples are tender and the tapioca is cooked.

Recommended variety - Bramley

BRAMLEY CRUNCH (serves 4)

1lb/450g apple purée, cooked with peeled zest of lemon (remove before blending)
6oz/175g demerara sugar
6oz/175g brown breadcrumbs
2oz/60g butter

Melt butter in frying pan, add breadcrumbs and sugar and stir over full heat until golden brown and crisp. Leave to cool.

Arrange alternate layers of purée and crumbs in tall sundae glasses. Top with whipped cream or yoghurt.

NB. The crunchy layer may be made with crushed digestive or ginger biscuits or crunchy breakfast cereal.

BAKED BRAMLEY APPLE (A quick and easy microwave dish)

8oz/225g Bramley apples (washed, cored and skin scored around the
circumference)
1 tablespoon sultanas
1 dessertspoon honey or golden syrup
Half tablespoon chopped walnuts
Half tablespoon chopped glace cherries

Place apples on dish and microwave for one minute on HIGH and one minute on
LOW.

Mix sultanas, cherries, honey or syrup and chopped nuts and pack into centre
of the apples. Microwave on HIGH for 30 seconds.

Allow to stand for 2 minutes and serve with whipped cream or yoghurt.

FAN OF POACHED PEARS

Allow 1 pear per person

Peel and halve the fruit, scoop out the core and coat with lemon juice to prevent discolouring. Poach the pears lightly for about 10-15 minutes until tender in a light sugar syrup, or red or rose wine which has been sweetened with a little honey. Drain well. Leaving the stalk end intact cut each pear half lengthwise into five slices and flatten gently to fan out. Garnish and serve with a little of the syrup poured over.

Recommended variety - Comice/Conference

FRESH PEARS

Concluding a meal with fresh fruit is always popular and this is one suggestion for using pears.

Peel, core and slice your dessert pears and sprinkle over with lemon juice to prevent discolouration. Before serving sprinkle over with caster sugar and a little kirsch or any other complementary liqueur of your choice.

PEARS IN WINE (suitable for diabetics)

2 ripe pears (peeled, halved and core scooped out)
Quarter pint/125ml rose or red wine
1 x 1"/25cm cinnamon stick
Strip of orange peel
3 tablespoons/45ml double cream (whipped)

Heat the wine in a pan with a base large enough to accommodate the four pear halves. Add the cinnamon stick and orange peel and simmer for 5-10 minutes, depending on the ripeness of the pears. Remove the cinnamon and orange peel and serve pears hot in individual bowls with the whipped cream.

Recommended variety - Comice

APPLE AND PEAR DESSERT (serves 4)

2 sheets of filo pastry
2oz/50g butter (melted)
2 ripe pears (peeled, quartered and cored)
2 dessert apples (peeled, quartered and cored)
Half pint/275ml water
Pared rind and juice of 1 lemon
3oz/75g sugar
1 blade of mace
2 sprigs of mint
6 cracked cardamom pods
4 mint sprigs to garnish

For the caramel syrup -
6oz/175g caster sugar
3fl.oz/75ml water

Set oven at 200C/400F/Gas Mark 6.

Lay filo pastry on a work surface, brush one sheet with the melted butter and top with the second sheet. Brush over the remaining butter. Cut out four circles or shapes to cover the bottom of your serving plates, place on a baking tray and bake for 10 minutes until golden brown. Leave to cool.

Sprinkle fruit with the lemon juice. Put the water, sugar, lemon rind, mace, mint and cardamom in a pan and bring to the boil stirring until the sugar is dissolved. Strain the syrup reserving the lemon rind. Place the pears and apples in another pan and pour over the strained syrup. Cover and simmer for 8-10 minutes or until all the fruit is tender and then drain. Cut the lemon rind into fine needle shreds.

To make the caramel syrup put the water and sugar in a pan and boil until the sugar dissolves. Continue boiling for a further 3 minutes, add the lemon shreds and continue to boil until the syrup is a light golden colour.

Arrange the filo shapes on serving plates, top each with 2 quarters of pears and apples and spoon over the caramel syrup. Decorate with mint sprigs.

Recommended variety - Comice/Conference

PEAR AND GINGER PUDDING

4oz/100g breadcrumbs
2oz/50g grated or shredded suet
1lb/450g pears (peeled and grated with the rind of 1 lemon)
4oz/100g sugar
1oz/25g chopped preserved ginger
1 x 2pt/1.1 litre pudding basin

Butter the pudding basin. Mix breadcrumbs with suet and add the sugar and chopped ginger to the grated pears. Put a layers as follows - one-third of the crumb mixture in, half the pear mixture, another one-third of the crumb mixture, a second layer of pears and top with the remaining crumb mixture. Cover bowl with greased paper and steam for 2 hours, topping up water with boiling water as necessary.

Recommended variety - Comice/Conference

DUCHESS PEARS (serves 4)

4 ripe pears (peeled, halved and cored)
1pt/575ml milk
Half inch/1cm cinnamon stick
2oz/50g ground rice
Half ounce/14g butter
A little red currant jelly
A few blanched almonds
2 tablespoons/30ml lemon syrup
1oz/25g caster sugar

Put milk in saucepan with the cinnamon and bring to the boil very slowly. Remove the cinnamon and pour the milk over the ground rice that has been mixed with a little cold milk. Return to the saucepan adding the butter and caster sugar and stir over a gently heat until quite thick. Leave to cool and turn into a glass dish.

Place pears flat side up on the rice and pour over the lemon syrup. Fill the centre of each half pear with the red currant jelly and place a blanched almond on each.

Recommended variety - Williams

NB. As an aternative you can use halves of fresh or canned peaches.

FRESH FRUIT COCKTAIL (serves 4)

1 ripe peach (peeled, stoned and cut into small slices)
I ripe pear (peeled, cored and sliced)
1 grapefruit (peeled and segments chopped)
2 tablespoons raspberries
1 banana (peeled and sliced)
1 tablespoon/15ml sherry (optional)
1 teaspoon/5ml lemon juice
A few grains of salt
4oz/100g caster sugar

Put all the prepared fruit with any juice into a basin. Mix together the wine, sugar, lemon juice and salt. Stir to dissolve the sugar and pour over the fruit mixture. Keep in a cool place until ready to serve.

Recommended variety - Comice

PEARS IN PORT (serves 4)

4-6 hard green pears (peeled, halved and cored)
6oz/175g granulated sugar
1pt/575ml water
Thinly pared rind of 1 lemon
4 tablespoons/60ml red port

Put water and sugar in a pan and heat slowly until sugar is dissolved. Add the lemon rind and pears and bring to the boil. Reduce heat and simmer gently until pears are almost tender. Pour in the port and continue to cook for a few more minutes. Remove pears from the cooking liquid with a slotted spoon, strain the liquid into a clean saucepan and boil fast to reduce to make a thick syrup. Pour over pears and leave to cool. Keep in refrigerator until ready to serve.

Recommended variety - cooking variety

HONEYED FRUIT SALAD (serves 4)

4oz/100g red cherries (washed and stoned)
4oz/100g raspberries
4oz/100g strawberries (hulled)
4oz/100g pears (peeled, cored and sliced)
4oz/100g dessert apples (peeled, cored and sliced)
2 tablespoons/30ml lemon juice
2 tablespoons/30ml clear honey
1pt/575ml water

Sprinkle sliced apples and pears with half the lemon juice to prevent discolouration. Heat the water and honey together to make a syrup, add the sliced apples and pears and poach very gently over a low heat for a few minutes until soft. Leave to cool.

Add the raspberries, strawberries and cherries, add 1 tablespoon/15ml of lemon juice and stir. Put fruit salad into a glass bowl and serve with pouring cream.

Recommended varieties - William pears and Discovery apples

GLAZED PEARS (serves 4)

4 pears (peeled, halved and cored)
1oz/25g butter
2oz/50g sugar
4fl.oz/100ml pouring cream

Set oven at 240C/475F/Gas Mark 9.

Place halved pears round side up in a lightly buttered baking dish and dot tops with the butter and sugar. Put in oven and watch closely as the pears become caramelized. Turn the oven down to a lower setting (150C/300F/Gas Mark 2). Pour cream over pears and leave in oven until very tender. Turn pears over and serve with a glace cherry in the centre of each pear.

Recommended variety - Comice/Conference

PEARS IN RED WINE

5-6 ripe dessert pears (peeled with stalks left intact)
5oz/150g sugar
Quarter pint/150ml water
Quarter pint/150ml red wine (claret or burgundy)
Strip of lemon rind
Small piece of stick cinnamon
1 teaspoon arrowroot
1oz/25g almonds
Whipped cream (optional)

To make the syrup, put the sugar, water, wine, lemon rind and cinnamon stick in a pan and bring to the boil slowly ensuring the sugar is dissolved and then boil for one minute. Remove the 'eye' from each pear and place stalk upwards in the syrup. Poach slowly in pan until they are tender. Allow at least 20-30 minutes to prevent them discolouring. Remove pears and strain syrup which should now be reduced to around half pint/275ml. Mix the arrowroot with a little water and add to the syrup. Return pan to the stove and stir until boiling; cook until liquid is clear.

Set oven at 180C/350F/Gas Mark 4. Blanch, skin and split the almonds in half lengthways and brown quickly in the oven.

Arrange the pears on a serving dish, spoon over the syrup and scatter the almonds on top. Serve cold.

Recommended variety - Comice/Conference/Concorde

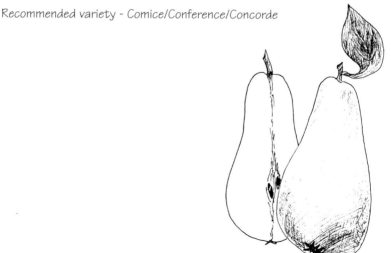

PEARS IN ORANGE CREAM

4-6 ripe pears (peeled, halved and cores scooped out)
Half pint/275ml water
2oz/50g granulated sugar

For the custard -
Half pint milk
2 egg yolks
1 teaspoon arrowroot
1 teaspoon caster sugar

For the orange cream -
1 large orange
5 sugar lumps
5fl.oz/150ml double cream
3fl.oz/75ml strained orange juice (use juice from orange and topped up with orange juice)

Put pears in a pan, rounded side down, with the water and sugar and cook gently until they are tender. Leave to cool in the syrup.

Shred the outer rind from half of the orange and cook in boiling water until tender. Drain and rinse well with cold water.

To prepare the custard, heat milk to near boiling, cream the egg yolks, arrowroot and sugar, add to the milk and bring to the boil. Stir over a gentle heat until the custard coats the back of a spoon but do not allow to boil. Strain and leave to cool.

Rub the sugar lumps over the remaining half of the orange to absorb the zest. Place lumps in a small basin, pour over the orange juice and stir until lumps are dissolved. Lightly whip the cream, stir in the orange syrup and cold custard.

Drain pears, arrange on a serving dish and coat with the orange cream. Sprinkle over the orange rind.

Recommended variety - Comice/Merton Pride

PEARS WITH CREAM

2lb/900g unripe dessert pears (peeled, cored and sliced)
Half ounce/14g butter
6oz/175g caster sugar
Piece of vanilla pod
4fl.oz/100ml thick cream

Using a shallow flameproof dish melt the butter and lay sliced pears in dish, preferably in one layer. Add the sugar and vanilla pod and simmer very gently until the pears are soft (about 5-20 minutes depending on ripeness of pears). Pour in cream and cook for a further 1-2 minutes, shaking the pan until the cream thickens.

Set oven at 180C/350F/Gas Mark 4. Transfer dish to a moderate oven for a few minutes until a golden skin has formed. Serve hot.

Recommended variety - Comice/Conference

HONEYED PEARS (serves 6)

6 medium pears (washed, halved and cores removed)
2fl.oz/50ml lemon juice
2fl.oz/50ml honey
1 teaspoon ground ginger
2 tablespoons/30ml cooking oil
12 whole cloves

Set oven at 180C/350F/Gas Mark 4.

Arrange pears in a shallow oiled casserole dish and put one clove into each half. Blend lemon juice, honey, ginger and oil together, pour over pears and bake for about 15 minutes. Fill centre of each pear with cottage or soy cheese. May be served hot or cold.

Recommended variety - Comice/Conference

NB. Peaches may also be used as an alternative.

PEAR FRITTERS WITH CARAMEL AND SESAME SEED COATING (serves 4)

2 eggs (beaten)
Quarter pint/150ml water
Quarter pint/150ml milk
6oz/175g wholemeal flour
Pinch of salt
4 large ripe pears (peeled, halved and cored)
Vegetable oil for frying

For the caramel -
6oz/175g raw cane sugar
2oz/50g butter
3fl.oz/75ml water
2oz/50g sesame seeds
Clear honey (to taste)
Mint leaves (to garnish)

To make the batter combine the beaten eggs with the milk, water salt and 4oz/100g of the flour until smooth. Leave to stand for 30 minutes. Cut pears into quarters if rather large and coat wedges with remaining flour, dip in the batter and fry in the preheated oil for 2 minutes until golden. Drain well.

To prepare the caramel, heat the sugar, butter and water in a saucepan in a pan until a sugar thermometer reads 150C/300F. Add the sesame seeds and dip the pears in the caramel for a few seconds on either side. As each fritter is removed dip quickly into a bowl of ice cubes to set the caramel. Arrange on a plate and decorate with the mint leaves. Serve with honey drizzled over.

If you like the caramel softer and less brittle leave fritters in the refrigerator for 3 hours before serving.

Recommended variety - Comice

NB. Sharp cooking apples or firm ripe peaches may be used as alternatives for this recipe.

PEARS IN SAFFRON AND LEMON (serves 4)

8 ripe dessert pears (peeled with cores removed)
1lb/450g sugar
1¹/₂pt/850ml water
Juice of 2 lemons
Pinch of saffron filaments
1oz/25g arrowroot

Using a pan large enough to hold the pears upright, dissolve sugar with the lemon juice over a medium heat. Bring to the boil, adding the saffron and the pears. Lower heat and poach pears very gently for about 20 minutes or until tender. Remove pears carefully and arrange on a large or individual serving dishes. Check the liquid and adjust to taste adding more lemon juice or sugar. Blend the arrowroot with a little water, add to the pear liquid and cook for 1-2 minutes or until the sauce is clear. Pass sauce through a fine sieve and leave to cool. Spoon sauce over the pears and garnish with mint or nasturtium flowers.

Recommended variety - Comice/Merton Pride

STUFFED PEARS (serves 4)

4 large pears (washed and cored from the base)
2oz/50g ground almonds
1oz/25g sugar
Half ounce/14g butter
1 large egg yolk

Mix the ground almonds, sugar, butter and egg yolk to form a paste and fill the cores with the mixture. Wrap each pear tightly in foil and put under a hot grill for about 30 minutes, or until pears are soft, turning over once.

Recommended variety - Comice

DEVON PEARS (serves 4)

4 large pears (peeled with stalks left intact)
1oz/25g blanched almonds split in half
2oz/50g caster sugar
Half pint/275ml red wine
2 cloves

Spike the pears with the almond halves. Put the sugar, wine and cloves in a pan which is large enough to hold the pears, and heat gently until sugar has dissolved. Add the pears, standing them upright in the pan, cover and simmer gently for about 15 minutes or until just tender. Baste with the liquid from time to time.

Transfer the pears, using a slotted spoon, to a serving dish. Turn up the heat under the liquid and boil fast until it is reduced by half. Pour over the pears and serve hot or cold with yoghurt or cream.

Recommended variety - Comice

PEARS IN CIDER (serves 6)

6 hard dessert pears (peeled but leave stalks intact)
4oz/100g sugar
Half pint/275ml sweet cider
Half pint/275ml water
Thinly pared rind of half a lemon
1oz/25g blanched almonds (cut into slivers)

Set oven at 150C/300F/Gas Mark 2.

Stand pears upright in a deep casserole dish and sprinkle with the sugar. Mix the cider and water, pour round the pears and add the lemon rind. Cover and cook until pears are tender - cooking time may be up to 4 hours. Leave pears in dish to cool before removing carefully and arranging with stalks up in a shallow serving dish. Press the almond slivers into the pears. Put the liquid in a small saucepan, removing the lemon rind first, and boil until the quantity is reduced by half. Pour the syrup over the pears and chill. Serve with thick cream.

Recommended variety - Warden (Black Worcester)/Catillac/Conference

PEARS WITH PRALINE

4-5 dessert pears (peeled, cored and leave stalks intact)
2oz/50g granulated sugar
6fl.oz/175ml water
Half split vanilla pod or few drops vanilla essence
Stale Victoria sponge or Madeira cake
Grand Marnier or kirsch (optional)

For the praline -
2oz/50g unblanched almonds
2oz/50g caster sugar

Cream -
Half pint/275ml double cream
1 egg white (whipped)
Caster sugar to sweeten

Make the syrup by mixing the sugar and water with the vanilla pod, bring to the boil and allow to simmer for 5 minutes. Remove the vanilla pod. Put pears in the pan and poach slowly for 10-15 minutes until tender. Leave to cool in the liquid.

To prepare the praline, put the almonds and sugar in a heavy-based saucepan and cook over a gentle heat allowing the sugar to melt and brown before stirring with a metal spoon. When the almonds are caramelised, continue to cook for 1-2 minutes to ensure they are thoroughly toasted through. Turn out the caramel into an oiled tin and leave to set and then grind through a cheese grater or nutmill. Keep in a screw-top jar until needed.

Cut out a round of sponge or cake to fit each pear, set on a dish and moisten with a little of the syrup. Sprinkle over the Grand Marnier or kirsch if desired. Drain the pears and set on the cake round. Whip the cream lightly, add the egg white, sweeten slightly and stir in 2-3 tablespoons of the praline. Pile on top of pears and sprinkle over some of the praline. Chill before serving.

Recommended variety - Comice/Conference/Concorde

PEARS WITH DAMSONS

8 ripe dessert pears (peeled, cored leaving stalk intact)
8oz/225g damsons (washed and stoned)
8oz/225g granulated sugar
15fl.oz/425ml water
1 vanilla pod
5fl.oz/150ml double cream

Put the sugar in a pan with the water and vanilla pod and dissolve over a gentle heat. Then boil steadily for 5 minutes to make 1pt/575ml of sugar syrup. Remove vanilla pod. Poach pears gently well soaked in the syrup for at least 15 minutes. Drain and arrange on a serving dish to cool.

Add the prepared damsons to the syrup and simmer gently until tender. Turn into a strainer and allow to drain, rubbing the damsons through. Dilute sieved damsons with a little of the syrup to give a good coating consistency. Chill well. Strain purée over the pears. Whip the cream and pipe round the edge of the serving dish.

Recommended variety - Williams/Comice

PEARS IN PASTRY (serves 4)

12oz/350g prepared puff pastry
4 ripe dessert pears (peeled with stalk and core removed taking care not to cut through pear)
1oz/25g granulated sugar
2 tablespoons/30ml brandy
1 egg (beaten)
6 tablespoons red currant jelly
Small piece of angelica (to decorate)

Set oven at 220C/425F/Gas Mark 7.

Divide pastry into four pieces and roll out thinly, large enough to each enclose one of the pears. Fill the cores of the pears with the sugar and brandy. Keeping each pear upright, shape pastry around each one leaving a small hole at the top. Brush with the beaten egg and decorate using the pastry trimmings. Brush again with the egg.

Cook wrapped pears for about 15-20 minutes until pastry is golden brown and crisp.

Meanwhile, beat the redcurrant jelly until smooth and runny, rub through a strainer into a small pan and heat gently. Pour a little of the warmed redcurrant jelly into each pear and top with a piece of angelica to resemble a stalk. Serve with whipped cream.

Recommended variety - Comice

PEAR CASSIS (serves 4-6)

4-6 ripe dessert pears (peeled, halved and cores scooped out)
3oz/75g granulated sugar
Half pint/275ml water
1 vanilla pod or 2-3 drops of vanilla essence
1 x 7oz/200g can of blackcurrants
Half ounce/14g arrowroot
Caster sugar (for dusting)

Dissolve sugar in pan, add the vanilla pod and boil for 5 minutes. Remove the vanilla pod and set aside. Add the vanilla essence at this stage if using. Put prepared pears into syrup with rounded end down, bring to the boil then reduce heat and leave to simmer very slowly until they appear almost transparent. Leave to cool in the covered pan.

Rub the blackcurrants through a fine sieve or purée in a liquidiser, measure and make up to three-quarters pint/425ml with the syrup from the pears. Put into a pan and heat gently. Mix the arrowroot with 2 tablespoons/30ml of the pear syrup, add to the blackcurrant mixture and stir until boiling.

Drain the pears, put into a serving dish and pour over the blackcurrant sauce, dusting the top with caster sugar to prevent a skin forming. Leave to cool.

Recommended variety - Comice/Concorde

PEAR BELLE HELENE

4-5 even size pears (peeled and cored carefully from flower end)
1pt/575ml water
4oz/100g sugar
1 vanilla pod (split)

For chocolate sauce -
6oz/175g block chocolate
Half pint/275ml water
3oz/75g granulated sugar
4 lumps sugar (optional)
1 orange (optional)

Make syrup by dissolving sugar in water in a shallow pan. Boil rapidly for two minutes. Put pears in the syrup and add the vanilla pod*, cover pan and poach gently for 20-30 minutes until tender. Leave to cool in the syrup.

To prepare the chocolate sauce, rub the sugar lumps over the orange until they are well soaked in the zest. Break up the chocolate, add the granulated sugar and simmer with the pan uncovered until the sauce is syrupy and will coat the back of a spoon. Draw pan aside and add the sugar lumps if used. Stir, reboil and leave to cool.

To serve, drain the pears, arrange on a serving dish and coat with the chocolate sauce.

*When poaching the pears the finely pared rind of the orange can be used instead of the vanilla pod.

Recommended variety - Comice/Concorde/Gorham

RICE PEARS

Half pint/275ml milk
Half ounce/14g sugar
Half ounce/14g rice
Apricot jam
Dessicated coconut
6 ripe dessert pears (peeled, halved and cored)
Half ounce/14g butter
Clove essence

Simmer the milk, rice, butter and sugar gently until it is a soft creamy mixture. Leave to cool and spread at the bottom of a glass dish. Stew pears gently in a little sugar and water with a few drops of clove essence. Arrange the cooked pears, rounded side down on the rice and in the centre of each put a teaspoonful of apricot jam. Sprinkle with dessicated coconut and serve.

Recommended variety - Williams

PEAR AND CHOCOLATE CRUMBLE (serves 4-6)

4 pears (peeled, cored and chopped)
4 plums (peeled, quartered and stones removed)
2fl.oz/50ml dry cider

For the crumble -
2oz/50g butter
4oz/100g flour
1oz/25g caster sugar
2oz/50g chocolate buttons

Set oven at 200C/400F/Gas Mark 6.

Put all the prepared fruit in a large saucepan with the cider, bring to the boil and poach over a gentle heat for 5 minutes to slightly soften. To make the crumble, rub the butter into the flour and sugar until the mixture resembles find breadcrumbs, roughly chop the buttons and stir into the crumble mixture. Lightly grease a 2pt/1.1 litre ovenproof dish, put in the fruit and cover with the crumble. Bake for 20 minutes or until golden brown.

Recommended variety - Williams and Victoria plums

GLAZED PEAR FLAN (serves 6)

3 large pears (peeled and halved)
2 tablespoons/30ml lemon juice
5oz/150g caster sugar
1"/2.5cm cinnamon stick
8fl.oz/225ml water
4fl.oz/100ml red wine
1 tablespoon/15ml apricot jam (sieved)
1lb/450g puff pastry
Flour for dusting
1 egg white (beaten)
1oz/25g flaked almonds

Set oven at 200C/400F/Gas Mark 6.

Toss pears in lemon juice to prevent browning. Put sugar, cinnamon and water in a pan and boil rapidly for 5 minutes. Add the pears and wine, reduce heat, cover and simmer for 10-15 minutes. Remove pears from pan and allow to cool.

To make the glaze, bring the cooking liquid to the boil and boil fast until reduced by half. Stir in the apricot jam and remove pan from heat.

Roll out pastry on a floured board to a rectangle and quarter-inch/6mm thick. Carefully score a smaller rectangle half-inch/12mm in from edge of the pastry. Transfer to a baking tray and brush with egg white. Slice and overlap the pears down the centre of the rectangle and brush with the glaze to prevent drying out. Bake for 25-30 minutes. Spoon the remaining glaze over the pears, sprinkle with the flaked almonds and serve with cream.

NB. Do not stir the glaze while it is boiling as it creates bubbles and the glaze becomes dull instead of clear. Use the glaze while still warm and runny.

Recommended variety - Comice/Conference

PEAR & BRANDY TART (serves 6-8)

4 dessert pears (peeled, halved and cored)
3 tablespoons/45ml lemon juice
5 tablespoons/75ml brandy
1oz/25g caster sugar
Quarter pint/150ml double cream

For the almond pastry -
8oz/225g flour
Pinch of salt
3oz/75g ground almonds
3oz/75g caster sugar
2 egg yolks (beaten)
6oz/175g unsalted butter (softened)

Set oven at 180C/350F/Gas Mark 4.

Place pear halves in a shallow ovenproof dish and sprinkle with lemon juice to prevent browning. Pour over 3 tablespoons/45ml of the brandy, cover and bake for 15-20 minutes until soft but still firm. Leave to cool. Drain the pears and set liquid aside.

To make the pastry, sieve the flour and salt on to a work surface, sprinkle with the ground almonds and make a well in the centre. Gradually add the sugar and egg yolks and then the butter. Knead lightly, wrap in cling film and chill in the fridge for 30 minutes. Roll out half the pastry and line a 9"/23cm flan tin and arrange the drained pears with the narrow ends to the centre. Roll out remaining pastry, cut out a 2"/5cm circle from the middle and cover the pears. Brush with water and sprinkle with sugar. Bake for 25-30 minutes or until pale gold at oven setting 200C/400F/Gas Mark 6. Whip the cream, beat in the cooking liquid with remaining brandy and spoon into the middle of the pie while hot.

Recommended variety - Comice/Concorde

UPSIDE DOWN PEARS (serves 6)

2 medium pears (peeled, halved and cores scooped out)
7oz/200g butter
3oz/75g demerara sugar
2 tablespoons/30ml golden syrup
6oz/175g caster sugar
3 eggs (separated)
Grated zest and juice of 1 lemon
5oz/150g self-raising flour

Set oven at 170C/325F/Gas Mark 3.

Cut pears lengthways into thick slices and poach gently in boiling water for 3 minutes or until just tender. Drain. Melt 1oz/25g of the butter in a pan with the demerara sugar and golden syrup and cook over a gentle heat until the sugar has almost dissolved. Pour over the bottom and sides of a 2¹/₂pt/1¹/₂litre pudding basin. When this begins to set arrange the pear slices around the sides of the basin, securing them with the caramel sauce. Place a round slice of pear in the bottom pushing down through the caramel with a wooden spoon. Beat the remaining butter with the caster sugar until light and fluffy. Beat in the egg yolks and lemon zest and then gently stir in the flour and lemon juice. Whisk the egg whites until stiff and fold thoroughly into the mixture. Pour mixture into the basin, smooth over top and bake for 45-55 minutes. Check to see if cooked by inserting a metal skewer as for a cake - it should come out clean. Turn out onto a warmed serving dish and serve hot with custard or fresh cream.

Recommended variety - Comice

FRESH PEAR COMPOTE

6 dessert pears (peeled, cored and sliced)
5oz/150g caster sugar
2 liqueur glasses of cognac, rum or kirsch

Place sliced pears in a glass dish, sprinkle with the sugar and pour over your chosen liqueur. Leave to stand for 1 hour before serving.

Recommended variety - Comice/Conference/Concorde

PEAR AND GINGER TART (SERVES 6)

1 ready baked pastry case or 1 9"/23cm tin lined with rich shortcrust pastry
2oz/50g sugar
1 tablespoon/15ml preserved ginger syrup
1lb8oz/675g pears (peeled, quartered and cored)
2 egg yolks
2 teaspoons cornflour
Half pint/275ml single cream (heated)
Half teaspoon vanilla essence
2oz/50g preserved ginger (drained and chopped)

If baking pastry case, set oven at 200C/400F/Gas Mark 6. Line pastry shell with foil and weigh down with dried beans; bake for 10 minutes. Leave to cool.

Reset oven at 170C/325F/Gas Mark 3. In a large saucepan dissolve 1oz/25g of the sugar in half pint/275ml of the water and stir in the ginger syrup. Put prepared pears in the syrup and poach gently for 15 minutes. Remove pears and set aside to cool.

In a small bowl beat the egg yolks with the remaining sugar and cornflour, stir in the heated cream and vanilla essence. Arrange the pears in the pastry case, scatter over the chopped ginger and pour custard mixture over the top. Bake for 45 minutes or until the custard is set. Serve warm.

Recommended variety - Comice/Conference/Concorde

PEAR MERINGUES

8 dessert pears (peeled, quartered and cored)
4 egg whites
15 lumps of sugar
3½oz/85g caster sugar
Few drops of vanilla essence

Set oven at 150C/300F/Gas Mark 2.

Cook pears in a little water with the sugar lumps and vanilla essence. When cooked lay pears in a baking dish. Whisk the egg whites to a stiff froth and spread over the pears. Sprinkle over the sugar and bake in a slow oven until golden brown.

Recommended variety - Comice/Merton Pride

FLAMING PEARS

10 dessert pears (peeled, quartered and cored)
7oz/200g caster sugar
Half liqueur glass of rum

Prepare pears as for the Pear Meringue recipe, using the sugar. Just before serving pour the hot rum over and add a lighted match. Serve when burning.

Recommended variety - Conference/Comice

ROSY PEARS

2lb/900g pears (peeled, halved and cored)
1lb/450g red currant jelly
2 egg whites
3¹/₂oz/85g almonds (finely chopped)
3¹/₂oz/85g nuts (finely chopped)
2oz/50g caster sugar

Set oven at 150C/300F/Gas Mark 2.

Using a large pan heat the red currant jelly with a little water, add the prepared pears and cook slowly. Drain the pears and arrange in an ovenproof dish. Return the liquid to the heat and cook until it becomes very thick, then pour it over the pears. Whisk the egg whites to a stiff froth, mix in the caster sugar, almonds and nuts. Spread over the fruit and bake in a slow oven until golden brown. Serve hot.

Recommended variety - Williams/Comice

SEMOLINA PEARS

1lb/450g pears (peeled, quartered and cored)
3¹/₂oz/85g semolina
1 pt/575ml milk
5oz/150g caster sugar
Few drops of vanilla essence
1 egg yolk (beaten)
1 tablespoon/15ml kirsch
4 macaroons

Put 3¹/₂oz/85g sugar and a little water in a pan, add the pears and cook gently until soft. Remove pears and leave to cool; add kirsch to the syrup and set aside. In a separate pan cook the semolina with the remaining sugar, milk and vanilla essence. When the semolina is cooked add the beaten egg yolk and pour into a mould. Arrange the cooked pears on top, sprinkle over the crushed macaroons and put in the oven until it browns. Serve hot with the syrup.

Recommended variety - Conference/Concorde

BAKED PEARS

Allow 1 dessert pear per person (peeled and cored carefully)
1oz/25g sugar per pear
Half ounce/14g butter per pear

Set oven at 150C/300F/Gas Mark 2.

Place pears in a baking dish with stalk end upwards. Fill centres of pears with the sugar and dot a little butter on top. Put a little water in the bottom of the dish and bake in a slow oven, basting frequently with the juice until the pears are soft.

Recommended variety - Comice. If using cooking pears such as Catliiac, Warden or Uvedale allow longer to cook.

APPLE AND HORSERADISH SAUCE - 1

Quarter pint/150ml cider vinegar
Juice of 1 lemon
1 heaped tablespoon sugar
Quarter teaspoon salt
2 medium cooking apples (peeled and cored)
1oz/25g grated horseradish

Put vinegar, lemon juice, sugar and salt in a large pan, bring to the boil and stir until the sugar dissolves. Remove pan from heat and grate the apples into it. Add the horseradish, put back on a low heat and cook for one minute stirring constantly. Allow to cool for a further minute, pour into pot and seal. Will keep for 2-3 months.

Recommended variety - Lord Derby/Dumelow's Seedling

APPLE AND HORSERADISH SAUCE - 2

2 medium cooking apples (peeled, cored and chopped)
2 tablespoons/30ml water
2 tablespoons/30ml soured cream
2 tablespoons/30ml grated horseradish

Put apples in saucepan with water, cover and set on a low heat for 15 minutes. Then beat them to a purée. Take pan from heat and beat in the soured cream and horseradish. Put sauce in bowl and allow to cool completely. Can be served with herrings, mackerel and cold salt beef.

Recommended variety - Lord Derby/Golden Noble

BAKED APPLE SAUCE

2-3 medium cooking apples (peeled, quartered and cored)
1 tablespoon/15ml water
A little sugar
Dash of butter

Put water in a 2 pint basin and fill with the apples. Cover basin and cook in hot oven (with your pork joint) for about one hour or until they are reduced to a pulp. Remove from oven and beat smooth with a wooden spoon adding the sugar and butter as desired. Serve immediately.

Recommended variety - Early Victoria/Bramley/Newton Wonder

APPLE SAUCE (OVEN TOP METHOD)

4 large cooking apples (peeled, cored and sliced)
Water for cooking
1 teaspoon sugar
1 teaspoon lemon juice
1oz/25g butter or margarine

Put apple slices in a saucepan with sufficient water to just moisten. Simmer very gently until reduced to a pulp and then stir in the sugar and lemon juice. Beat in the butter with a wooden spoon until the sauce is smooth. Serve cold.

Recommended variety - Bramley/Newton Wonder/Lord Derby

CRANBERRY AND APPLE JELLY

2¼lb/1kg apples (sliced, do not peel or core)
1½lb/675g cranberries
Granulated sugar (quantity will have to be adjusted - see recipe instructions)

Put sliced apples and cranberries into pan with enough water to cover.
Simmer gently until thoroughly mashed. Strain through a sterilised jelly bag
and leave to drip for one hour. Check quantity and return to a cleaned pan.
Add sugar allowing 1¾lb/800g per 1¾pints/1 litre of extracted mixture.
Stir over a low heat until sugar is dissolved and then boil steadily until
setting point is reached. To test for this, spoon a little of the syrup onto
a cold saucer (as for jam), leave to cool and then run finger over the surface.
If it wrinkles it is ready. Remove the jelly from the heat and skim.
Pot in warm, sterilised jars, cover and label. Store in a cool, dry place.

Recommended variety - Bramley or try any windfalls

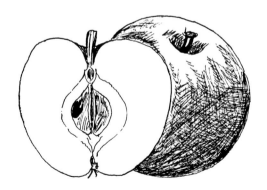

APPLE CAKE

6oz/175g self-raising flour
3oz/75g margarine or lard
6oz/175g peeled, cored and diced apples
3oz/75g sugar
Milk

Set oven at 190C/375F/Gas Mark 5.

Rub the fat into the flour and add the diced apple. Sprinkle over the sugar and mix together with a little milk to make a very firm dough. Roll out the mixture or if a bit sticky press out to form a round about 7"-8"/175-200mm across. Put on a greased baking sheet and bake for 20 minutes at above temperature and then reduce heat to 170C/325F/Gas Mark 3 for a further 20 minutes.

Split open, butter well and eat hot. Can also be eaten as a pudding and served with custard or single cream.

Recommended variety - Cox/Worcester Pearmain

AUSTRALIAN SPICED APPLE CAKE

4oz/100g butter
4oz/100g sugar
3oz/75g cooked apple (sieved and unsweetened)
1 teaspoon of bicarbonate of soda
6oz/175g plain flour
Quarter teaspoon grated nutmeg
Quarter teaspoon ground cinnamon
3oz/75g seedless raisins or sultanas

Set oven at 150C/300F/Gas Mark 2.

Cream the butter and sugar together well. Stir the bicarbonate of soda into the apple and add to the creamed mixture. Sift the flour and spices together and add to the mixture, adding the raisins or sultanas and mixing well. Grease and line a 7"/18cm cake tin, spoon in mixture and bake for 55-60 minutes.

Recommended variety - Bramley/Lord Derby

APPLE AND BANANA BREAD

1 medium size apple (chopped)
1lb/450g wholemeal flour
Half ounce/14g yeast
Quarter pt/150ml water
2oz/50g raw brown sugar
1 teaspoon salt
1 teaspoon ground cinnamon
1 teaspoon ground nutmeg
2oz/50g sultanas
2 small bananas (mashed)
Grated rind of half a lemon

Set oven at 190C/375F/Gas Mark 5.

Steam the apple until tender and press through sieve to make a purée.
Leave to cool. Mix together 4oz/100g of the flour, yeast and warm water until
smooth and leave in a warm place until frothy. Mix the remaining flour, sugar,
salt, spices and sultanas in a bowl and stir in the yeast mixture, apple purée,
mashed banana and lemon and beat well. Divide the mixture between two
greased 1lb/450g loaf tins. Leave to prove in a warm place until the mixture
reaches the top of the tin. Bake for about 35 minutes.

Recommended variety - Bramley

APPLE BUNS

2 medium sized cooking apples (cored and diced)
8oz/225g wholemeal flour
Pinch of salt
Half teaspoon ground cinnamon
1 teaspoon baking powder
6oz/175g butter or margarine
2oz/50g raw brown sugar
1 egg (beaten)

Set the oven to 190C/375F/Gas Mark 5.

Combine the flour, salt, spice and baking powder in a bowl. Rub in the butter or
margarine until mixture resembles fine crumbs and then add the remaining
ingredients, mixing well together. Place heaped spoonfuls on to a lightly
greased baking tray and bake for 20-25 minutes until golden. Cool slightly
before transferring to a wire tray.

Recommended variety - Lord Derby/Bramley

APPLE SAUCE CAKE

3 apples (peeled, cored and roughly chopped)
Half tablespoon lemon juice
4fl.oz/100ml water
Half ounce/14g butter
6oz/175g raisins
2oz/50g hazelnuts
1 small bottle maraschino cherries (thoroughly drained)
1 teaspoon bicarbonate of soda
4fl.oz/100ml rendered chicken fat or vegetable oil
8oz/225g light brown sugar
7oz/200g plain white flour
Half teaspoon salt
1 teaspoon ground cinnamon
Half teaspoon ground nutmeg
Quarter teaspoon powdered cloves

Set the oven at 180C/350F/Gas Mark 4.

To make the apple sauce put the apples in a saucepan with the lemon juice
and water, bring to the boil and simmer until the apples are soft
(about 15 minutes). Beat well to reduce apples to a purée and then stir
in the butter. This should give you about 8oz/225g of apple sauce.
Set this aside.

Mix the raisins, nuts and cherries and put them through a mincer or
chop finely in a food processor, ensuring they are well mixed but not a
paste like mixture. Set aside.

In a large bowl stir the bicarbonate of soda and apple sauce together,
stir in the fat or oil and the sugar. Mix in the flour, salt and spices and
finally add the ground fruit and nut mixture. Mix thoroughly. Put mixture
into a greased 8"/20cm square cake tin and bake for 1 to 1¼ hours
when a metal skewer inserted into the middle should come out clean.
Allow the cake to cool in the tin for 10 minutes and then turn it on to
a wire rack to cool completely.

Recommended variety - Bramley

AMERICAN APPLE SAUCE CAKE

1¼lb/550g cooking apples (peeled, cored and chopped)
2 tablespoons/30ml water
4oz/100g butter or margarine
6oz/175g sugar
1 teaspoon/5ml vanilla essence
1 egg
1lb/450g plain flour
Half teaspoon ground cinnamon
1 teaspoon ground mixed spice
Half teaspoon ground cloves
1½ teaspoons bicarbonate of soda
8oz/225g raisins
8oz/225g pecan nuts (roughly chopped)

Set the oven to 180C/350F/Gas Mark 4.

Cook the apples with the water until they are reduced to a purée (for the sauce), beat well until smooth and leave to cool completely.

Beat the butter or margarine with the sugar until pale and soft, beat in the vanilla essence, cooled apple purée and egg. Sift the flour, spices and bicarbonate of soda, stir in the raisins and nuts and then add these dry ingredients to the apple mixture. Spoon into a well greased loose-bottomed 8"/20cm cake tin. Level surface and bake for about one and a half to one and three-quarter hours. Check the cake after one and a quarter hours, if it is browning lay a piece of foil over the top. When cooked, a metal skewer inserted into the cake should come out clean. Allow to cool in the tin for two minutes, turn out and leave on wire rack to cool completely.

If desired, the cake can be served warm with cream and extra apple sauce.

Recommended variety - Mother/Bramley

DANISH APPLE CAKE

2lb/900g cooking apples (peeled, cored and chopped)
2 tablespoons/30ml water
3oz/75g sugar
3oz/75g melted butter
Grated rind of 1 lemon
8oz/225g dry very lightly browned breadcrumbs
2oz/50g demerara sugar

Set the oven on 190C/375F/Gas Mark 5.

Cook the apples with the water, sugar and lemon rind until they are reduced to a purée. Boil for a few minutes to thicken the mixture, remove from heat and beat thoroughly. Grease generously with some of the butter and base-line a deep 8"/20cm cake tin. Mix the breadcrumbs with the sugar, then layer with the apple purée in the tin, starting and ending with crumbs. Pour the remaining butter over the top and bake for about 30 minutes or until top is golden brown.

If serving hot, turn out immediately. If serving cold, leave in the tin until warm and then turn out on to wire rack and allow to cool completely.

Recommended variety - Dumelow's Seedling/Bramley

ENGLISH APPLE CAKE

12oz/350g plain flour
3 teaspoons baking powder
4oz/100g butter or margarine
4oz/100g sugar
1 teaspoon ground mixed spice
Half teaspoon ground cloves
6oz/175g cooking apples (peeled, cored and grated)
2fl.oz/50ml medium sweet cider

Set the oven on 190C/375F/Gas Mark 5.

Sift the flour and baking powder into a bowl, rub in the butter or margarine until the mixture resembles fine breadcrumbs. Stir in the sugar and spices, add the grated apples and mix well. Stir in the cider to make a stiff mixture. Turn mixture into a well-greased 2lb/900g loaf tin and bake for about 1 hour or until risen, golden on top and firm to the touch. A skewer inserted into the cake should come out clean. Leave in tin for a few minutes and then turn out onto a wire rack.

Serve cut into thick slices and buttered. This cake is good warm or cold.

Recommended variety - Bramley

APPLE CREAM BUNS (makes 16)

2oz/50g butter
Quarter pint/150ml water
2¹/2oz/65g plain flour
2 eggs (beaten)
1lb/450g apples (peeled, cored and sliced)
1oz/25g sugar
5fl.oz/150ml fresh double cream
Icing sugar

Set oven at 200C/400F/Gas Mark 6.

To make pastry - put water and butter into a medium saucepan and allow
to heat slowly until butter melts. Then bring to a brisk boil. Lower the heat
and tip in all the flour and salt, stirring briskly until mixture forms a soft
ball and leaves the side of the pan. Remove from the heat and allow to cool
slightly. Gradually add the beaten eggs, a little at a time, beating until
the mixture is smooth and shiny. Spoon 16 buns onto a buttered baking
sheet and cook for 10 minutes. Remove from the oven and make a slit in
the side of each cake. Return to the oven for a further 5 minutes.
Cool buns on a wire rack.

Poach the apple slices in quarter pint/150ml of water with the sugar for 15
minutes, until soft and leave to cool. Whip the cream until stiff peaks form.
Remove the apple slices from the syrup with a slotted spoon and then fold
them in the whipped cream. Split the buns, fill them with the apple mixture
and dust with sifted icing sugar.

Recommended variety - Bramley

SOMERSET APPLE CAKE

3oz/75g butter
6oz/175g caster sugar
1 orange rind (grated)
8oz/225g self raising flour
1lb/450g apples (peeled, cored and cubed)
2 eggs (beaten)
2 tablespoons/30ml milk
1oz/25g candied peel
1oz/25g granulated sugar

Set oven at 180C/350F/Gas Mark 4.

Grease and flour a 9"/23cm cake tin.

Cream butter and orange rind, add the caster sugar and beat until light and creamy. Mix one tablespoon/25g of the flour with the apples in a dish. Put eggs and milk in a bowl with the creamed butter. Add the remaining flour, candied peel and apples to the creamed mixture and blend well, using a metal spoon. Turn into cake tin and sprinkle with the granulated sugar. Bake for 40-50 minutes until golden brown.

Can be served cold as a cake or hot as a pudding with cream.

Recommended variety - Bramley

APPLE FRUIT CAKE

1lb/450g cooking apples (peeled, cored and roughly sliced)
Water
8oz/225g plain flour
1 level teaspoon bicarbonate of soda
1 level teaspoon powdered cinnamon
Half teaspoon mixed spice
Half teaspoon ground ginger
6oz/175g sultanas
2oz/50g chopped peel
2oz/50g seedless raisins
2oz/50g chopped walnuts
2oz/50g chopped glacé ginger
5oz/150g butter
6oz/175g soft brown sugar
Rind of 1 lemon finely grated
2 eggs
Caster sugar

Set oven at 170C/325F/Gas Mark 3.

Cook apples until quite soft using minimum amount of water
(1-2 tablespoons/15-30ml). Sieve or liquidise cooked apples.
Measure 8fl.oz/225ml out of the apple purée.

Grease and line the base of an 8"/20cm round cake tin.

Sieve together the flour, bicarbonate of soda, cinnamon, mixed spice and
ginger. Add the sultanas, peel, raisins, walnuts and glacé ginger and mix
thoroughly. In another bowl cream the butter, brown sugar and lemon rind
and then beat in the eggs. Fold into this mixture the dry ingredients
alternately with the apple purée. Put in tin, dredge top with the caster
sugar. Bake in centre of oven for about one and a quarter hours.

Recommended variety - Bramley

APPLE MUFFIN

8oz/225g plain flour
1 teaspoon baking powder
3oz/75g fat
2oz/50g sugar
3 apples (peeled, cored and grated)
1 egg
Milk

Set oven at 220C/425F/Gas Mark 7.

Rub the fat into the flour, adding the baking powder and sugar. Add the grated apples and bind the mixture with the egg and sufficient milk to form a dough. Spread mixture on a greased flat baking tin and bake for about 30 minutes. Remove from oven and cut into squares, split each square and spread with butter, sprinkle with sugar and serve at once.

Recommended variety - Bramley

APPLE RAISIN LOAF

4oz/100g margarine
8oz/225g sugar
2 eggs
4oz/100g chopped nuts
8oz/225g chopped raisins
12oz/350g plain flour
1 teaspoon baking powder
1 teaspoon mixed spice
About 8oz/225g stewed apples
Quarter teaspoon salt

Set oven at 170C/325F/Gas Mark 3.

Cream the margarine and the sugar. Beat in the eggs, add the flour, spice, baking powder and salt alternately with the stewed apples. Add the nuts and raisins and mix well. Grease a loaf tin (8 x 5"/20 x 13cm), pour in mixture and bake for about 1^{1}/2 hours.

Recommended variety - Bramley/Dumelow's Seedling

APPLE CHEESE CAKES

4oz/100g short pastry
8oz/225g apples (peeled, cored and sliced)
3 cloves
1oz/25g margarine
3oz/75g sugar
2 eggs

Set oven at 230C/450F/Gas Mark 8.

Line some patty tins with the pastry. Stew the apples with the sugar and cloves until soft, add the margarine and beat it well in. Rub the mixture through a sieve. Beat the eggs into the apple purée and put a teaspoon of mixture into each patty tin. Bake for 20 minutes.

If preferred, grated lemon rind can be substituted for the cloves.

Recommended variety - Newton Wonder

APPLE AND CHEESE SCONE ROUND

1 large cooking apple (peeled, cored and grated)
12oz/350g wholemeal flour
A little lemon juice
Pinch of salt
1 tablespoon salt
3oz/75g butter or margarine
3oz/75g caster sugar
Quarter pint/150ml milk (preferably sour)
2oz/50g grated cheese
A little extra milk

Set the oven at 200C/400F/Gas Mark 6.

Sprinkle grated apple with lemon juice to prevent browning. This also adds to the flavour. Sieve flour, salt and baking powder together and rub in the butter or margarine until the mixture resembles fine breadcrumbs. Stir in the caster sugar and grated apple. Mix to a stiff dough with the milk. Turn dough onto a floured board and make into a round about 1/2"/12mm thick. Brush the top with milk and sprinkle over the grated cheese.
Mark the round into eight wedges. Bake for 25 minutes or until golden brown. Best served warm and buttered in the middle.

Recommended variety - Bramley

APPLE GINGERBREAD WITH CINNAMON ICING - 1

2oz/50g butter or margarine
2oz/50g soft brown sugar
3oz/75g black treacle or syrup
4oz/100g plain flour
12oz/350g cooking apples (peeled, cored and chopped finely)
1 teaspoon ground ginger
Half teaspoon bicarbonate of soda
Half teaspoon ground cloves
A little milk to mix
8"/20cm shallow cake tin (greased)

For the icing -
Half teaspoon cinnamon
8oz/225g icing sugar

Set oven at 180C/350F/Gas Mark 4.

Melt the butter, sugar and syrup over a gentle heat. Remove from heat and blend in the sifted flour, ginger, bicarbonate of soda and cloves. Mix in the apples and then the milk to make a soft dropping consistency. Spoon into the cake tin and bake for 1 hour. Leave cake to cool and turn out, making sure it is completely cold before icing.

Mix the icing sugar with a little water and the cinnamon to a coating consistency and top the gingerbread with the glaze.

Recommended variety - Bramley

APPLE GINGERBREAD WITH CINNAMON ICING - 2

8oz/225g cooking apples (peeled, cored and sliced)
3oz/75g demerara sugar
4oz/100g golden syrup
3oz/75g butter
6oz/175g self raising flour
1 teaspoon ground ginger
Quarter teaspoon ground gloves
1 egg

For the icing -
6oz/175g icing sugar
2-3 dessertspoons/25ml hot water
1 level teaspoon ground cinnamon

Set oven at 170C/325F/Gas Mark 3.

Put apples in a pan with a dessertspoonful of sugar and sufficient water to keep them from burning. Stew gently until tender and then mash and leave to cool. Put golden syrup in pan with the butter and the remainder of the sugar, dissolve slowly and leave to cool.

Sift flour into a basin with the ground ginger and ground cloves. In a separate bowl whisk up the egg, add the dissolved syrup mixture and mix well together. Add the flour, mix well, stir in the apple pulp and continue to fully mix all ingredients. Turn mixture into a well greased loaf tin and bake for about half an hour. When cooked leave in tin for a while before turning out.

To make icing topping, mix sugar and cinnamon through a sieve and gradually add hot water to make a thick coating. Spread over the cooled gingerbread and leave to set.

Recommended variety - Lord Derby/Bramley

DORSET APPLE CAKE

1lb/450g cooking apples (peeled, cored and finely chopped)
1lb/450g plain flour
8oz/225g margarine or butter
8oz/225g sugar
Pinch of salt
3 teaspoons baking powder
Milk

Set oven at 180C/350F/Gas Mark 4.

Rub margarine or butter into the flour and add the salt and baking powder. Mix the sugar and chopped apple and stir into the flour. Add milk carefully until you have a firm dough. Pat into a flat cake about 3/4"/20mm thick. Bake in a round flat tin for about three quarters to one hour.
Cut open, butter well and eat hot.

Recommended variety - Newton Wonder/Bramley

NORWEGIAN APPLE CAKE

4oz/100g plain flour
1 teaspoon baking powder
1 teaspoon cinnamon (optional)
2oz/50g margarine
4oz/100g caster sugar
1 egg
3fl.oz/75ml milk
1 eating apple (peeled, cored and thinly sliced)

Set oven at 180C/350F/Gas Mark 4.

Grease and line a 7"/18cm square tin. Whisk the egg and sugar until thick and creamy. Heat milk in a pan and melt the margarine. Stir the milk and margarine gently into the whisked mixture, fold in the flour, baking powder and cinnamon, using a metal spoon. Arrange the apple in the bottom of the tin and cover with the mixture. Bake for 20 minutes or until firm and golden brown. Serve hot or cold in slices with cream.

Recommended variety - Bramley/Blenheim Orange

APPLE AND BANANA PIECES

2 dessert apples (peeled, cored and coarsely grated)
2 ripe bananas
6oz/175g light soft brown sugar
4oz/100g soft margarine
2 large eggs (beaten)
8oz/225g self-raising flour
2 teaspoons ground cinnamon
2oz/50g chopped walnuts
A little sifted icing sugar

Set oven at 190C/375F/Gas Mark 5.

Brush a 12"x9"/304x228mm swiss roll tin with melted fat and line the base with greaseproof paper; brush the lining also. Put grated apples in a bowl, add the peeled bananas and mash them together with a fork. Add the sugar, margarine, eggs, sifted flour, cinnamon and chopped walnuts and, using a wooden spoon, mix thoroughly together. Beat for a minute then spoon into the tin, spreading evenly to the sides. Bake for 30 to 35 minutes or until golden brown. Leave cake in tin to cool then cut into pieces. Place on a wire rack and dust with icing sugar. (Makes about 18).

Recommended variety - Cox/Worcester Pearmain

APPLE SLICE SQUARES

4oz/100g self-raising flour
4oz/100g margarine
4oz/100g caster sugar
2 large eggs (beaten)
Few drops almond essence
2 eating apples (peeled, cored, quartered and sliced into 36 slices)
1oz/25g demerara sugar

Set oven at 180C/350F/Gas Mark 4.

Lightly grease a 13"x9"/330x228mm tin with melted fat, line the base with greaseproof paper and brush with fat also. Beat the margarine until soft, add the sugar and cream together. Gradually add the eggs, stirring well after each addition, then add the almond essence. Sift the flour, and using a wooden spoon, stir into the creamed mixture. Spread mixture evenly over the base of the tin and arrange sliced apple on the top. Sprinkle top with the demerara sugar and bake for 40 minutes or until golden brown. Allow to cool slightly in the tin and then cut into squares (makes approximately 12). Transfer to a wire rack to cool completely.

Recommended variety - Cox

APPLE AND RAISIN CAKE

1lb/450g apples (cooked and puréed to make 1/2 pint/275ml liquid)
12oz/350g plain flour
Pinch of salt
1 1/2 level teaspoons bicarbonate of soda
6oz/175g margarine
6oz/175g caster sugar
1 teaspoon ground cinnamon
2oz/50g chopped walnuts
6oz/175g seedless raisins
Quarter pint/150ml milk
1oz/25g demerara sugar

Set oven at 170C/325F/Gas Mark 3.

Use a small roasting tin - about 7"x10"/177x255mm. Lightly grease tin, line
base with greaseproof paper and grease paper also. Sieve the flour, salt,
bicarbonate of soda and cinnamon, add the margarine cut into small pieces
and rub in with fingertips until mixture resembles fine breadcrumbs. Stir in the
sugar, walnuts and raisins and then bind these with the apple purée and milk to
make a stiff consistency. Turn mixture into tin, level surface and sprinkle over
with the demerara sugar. Bake for one and a quarter hours or until mixture is
springy to touch. Cool cake on a wire tray and store in an airtight tin for at
least a day before serving.

Recommended variety - Bramley

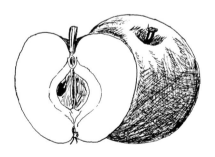

OATMEAL APPLE TORTE

2oz/50g butter or margarine
3oz/75g sugar
1 small egg (beaten)
2oz/50g plain flour
Half teaspoon baking powder
Pinch salt
Half teaspoon ground cinnamon
Pinch ground nutmeg
Pinch ground cloves
1 teaspoon cocoa (optional)
4oz/100g chopped apples (about half inch/1cm square)
Half ounce/14g chopped walnuts
Grated rind of half a lemon
2oz/50g rolled wheat or oats

Set oven at 170C/325F/Gas Mark 3.

Cream butter or margarine with the sugar until light and fluffy, add the egg and blend well. Sift the flour, baking powder, salt, spices and cocoa (if using) and add to the sugar mixture, mixing until smooth. Add the apples, nuts, lemon rind and cereal and blend well. Put mixture in a greased pan and bake for about 20-25 minutes or until cooked through and golden brown. Leave to cool in pan and cut into portions.

Recommended variety - Bramley

APPLE TOPPED BAKE

Juice of 1 orange (about 4 tablespoons/60ml)
6oz/175g margarine
2oz/50g demerara sugar
6oz/175g golden syrup
3oz/75g medium oatmeal
3oz/75g self-raising flour
Pinch of salt
1 cooking apple (peeled, cored and grated)
Sprinkling of caster sugar
1 teaspoon finely grated orange rind

Set oven at 170C/325F/Gas Mark 3.

Generously grease a swiss roll tin 12"x8" (304x203mm). Put orange juice,
margarine, demerara sugar and golden syrup in a pan and heat gently until
melted. Sift the flour with pinch of salt and stir into the melted mixture with
the oatmeal. Spread mixture evenly into the prepared tin and bake for about
twenty minutes or until top is set firmly enough to hold the grated apple. Mix
grated apple with the orange rind, sprinkle over surface of part baked cake and
top with caster sugar. Return it to the oven for ten or fifteen minutes.
Cut into squares when cold.

Recommended variety - Bramley

PEAR BREAD (recipe for 1 loaf)

Half ounce/14g fresh yeast*
2 tablespoons/30g sugar
2oz/50g honey
2oz/50g butter
4fl.oz/100ml milk
12oz/350g flour
Salt
1 egg (lightly beaten)
12oz/350g dried pears (chopped)
4oz/100g sultanas
Grated rind and juice of half a lemon
1 teaspoon ground cinnamon
Port wine
2oz/50g chopped walnuts or pecan nuts
Sweetened milk to glaze

If using fresh yeast, put in a small bowl and mash, add half teaspoon sugar and 2 tablespoons/30ml lukewarm water. Set aside in a warm place for 15 minutes or until the yeast is puffed up and frothy. *If using dried yeast make up as per instructions on packet.

While yeast is working, melt the honey and butter in the milk - the mixture should be no hotter than lukewarm. Sift the flour with the salt into a warmed bowl, make a well in the centre and pour in the frothy yeast, the milk mixture and the egg. Using fingers, mix the flour and liquid together to form a soft dough, adding more liquid if the dough is too dry or more flour if too sticky. Pat dough into a ball and turn onto a floured surface, kneading well for 10 minutes. Make a ball of the dough and place in a lightly greased bowl. Cover with a greased polythene bag and set aside in a warm place for one hour or until the dough doubles in size.

Meanwhile, put the pears, sultanas, remaining sugar, lemon rind and juice and cinnamon in a saucepan, add quarter pint/150ml of port wine and simmer the mixture, stirring frequently for 20 minutes or until the fruit is mushy. Add more wine if necessary to keep the fruit cooking without sticking to the pan. The mixture should be very thick and moist. Stir in the nuts and set aside to cool.

Turn dough onto a floured surface and knead it for 2 minutes. Roll into a rectangle about quarter inch/half cm thick. Spread the filling over the dough, leaving a 1"/2cm border round edge. Fold the longer sides of the rectangle over the filling and roll from the shorter side to make a swiss roll.

Transfer roll to baking sheet and set aside in a warm place for 1 hour.

Set oven at 200C/400F/Gas Mark 6.

Brush top of the roll with the sweetened milk and bake for 10 minutes.
Reduce oven to 180C/350F/Gas Mark 4 and bake for a further 50 minutes.

Allow bread to cool completely before serving.

NB. This sweet milk bread can be served with tea or coffee.

• Most dessert pears can be dried when in season and stored to be used in the above or other recipes.

APPLE AND CABBAGE

Put 3 parts apple juice and 1 part cabbage juice into a liquidizer and blend for a few seconds.

WATERCRESS, TOMATO AND APPLE

Measure 1 part each of watercress juice and tomato juice and 2 parts apple juice into a liquidizer and blend for a few seconds.

WASSAIL

6 cooking apples (cored but not peeled)
Soft brown sugar (sufficient to fill centres of cored apples)
Half ounce/14g ground ginger
Half a grated nutmeg
Pinch of powdered cinnamon
8oz/225g Demerara sugar
3pt/1700ml ale, mild or brown
Half bottle of raisin wine or quarter bottle sherry
1 lemon
10 lumps of sugar

Set oven to 325F/170C/Gas Mark 3.

Roast apples in oven for 45-60 minutes taking care not to burst the skins.

In a saucepan mix together the ginger, nutmeg, cinnamon and sugar. Add 1pt/575ml of the ale and bring to the boil. Stir in the rest of the ale, the wine and 10 lumps of sugar that have been rubbed on the rind of the lemon. Heat the mixture but do not allow to boil. Put the roasted apples in a bowl, pour in the hot ale mixture with half the peeled and sliced lemon. Serve immediately.

Recommended variety - Bramley

MAKE YOUR OWN CIDER

3lb/1350g windfall cooking apples (washed thoroughly, bad bits cut out, peeled and cored)
3 really juicy lemons
2lb/900g granulated sugar
12pt/6.8litres cold water

Cut apples into small pieces and mince. Put into a clean plastic bucket if you have no large earthenware crock. Pour over water and leave covered for 7 days, stirring thoroughly every morning and night. Strain into a clean container and stir in the sugar, the lemon juice and finely grated lemon rind. Leave to stand for a further 24 hours. Strain into glass bottles with screw tops well secured.

Recommended variety - Lord Derby/Bramley

APPLE FIZZ (serves 2)

3 tablespoons/45ml apple purée
1 tablespoon/15ml lemon juice
2 scoops vanilla ice cream
Half pint/275ml lemonade

Liquidise or blend all ingredients together.
Pour into tall glasses and add ice cubes.

Recommended variety - Bramley

APPLE MILK SHAKE (serves 2)

2 tablespoons/30ml apple purée
2 teaspoon honey
Half pint/275ml milk
1 scoop vanilla ice cream
Place all ingredients in a liquidiser or use a blender to combine.
Pour into tall glasses, and top with additional ice cream. Add ice cubes.

Recommended variety - Bramley

APPLE WINE

2 gallons cider
4lb/1825g sugar

Place the cider in a small cask or bottle and add the sugar. Stir until the sugar has dissolved. Close loosely and leave to stand in a cool, dry place for 12 months.

APPLE TEA

2lb/900g apples (washed, quartered and cored)
2¹/₂oz/50g sugar
4 pints/2.3litres water
A few drops of vanilla essence or some cinnamon

Put vanilla or cinnamon in the water and bring to the boil. Add the apples and boil for ³/4 hour. Pass mixture through sieve, add the sugar and leave to get cold.

Recommended variety - Bramley

APPLE PRESERVE

10lb/4$\frac{1}{2}$kg apples - can be mixed varieties (peeled, cored and quartered)
10lb/4$\frac{1}{2}$kg sugar
3 teaspoons/15ml vanilla essence

Put apples in large preserving pan with the sugar, vanilla essence and one glass of water and cook on a very low heat for several hours until the apples are cooked. Some apples will go pulpy while others will still be in quarters. Put into clean, warmed jars and put on lids (as for jam). Will store for several months. When using turn out contents and serve with either ice cream or fresh cream.

Recommended varieties - see above

APPLE PICKLE

6lb/2$\frac{3}{4}$kg apples (peeled, cored and chopped into cubes)
3pt/1500ml vinegar
12 shallots (chopped)
12oz/350g sugar
1oz/25g turmeric
Half ounce/14g ground ginger
Half ounce/14g mustard
12 cloves and peppercorns (tied in a muslin bag)
Salt

Spread apple cubes on a dish and strew over with a little salt. Leave for 24 hours and then drain. Put into a large preserving pan the vinegar, shallots, sugar, turmeric, ground ginger, mustard and muslin bag. Boil for 10 minutes, remove the muslin bag and then add the drained apple chunks. Cook for 15 minutes or until tender but not mashed down. Put into warm sterlized jars and seal.

Recommended variety - Bramley Seedlings

APPLE AND TOMATO CHUTNEY

1lb/450g apples (peeled, cored and chopped finely)
1lb/450g onions (peeled and chopped finely)
1lb/450g ripe tomatoes (skinned and sliced)
Half pint/275ml vinegar
8oz/225g very dark brown sugar
Half ounce/14g mixed pickling spice (tied in a muslin bag)
1 teaspoon salt
4oz/100g sultanas
4oz/100g mustard seeds (if liked)

Mix all the ingredients in a large preserving pan, bring to the boil and simmer for about 4 hours. Remove the muslin bag and pot mixture in warm sterlized jars. Cover.

Recommended variety - Newton Wonder/Lord Derby

GREEN TOMATO AND APPLE CHUTNEY - 1

2lbs/900g green tomatoes (peeled and cut into quarters)
2lbs/900g cooking apples (peeled, cored and sliced)
1lb/450g shallots or onions (peeled and sliced)
6 red chillies
2oz/50g garlic (finely chopped)
12oz/350g sultanas
Half ounce/14g ground ginger
8oz/225g demerara sugar
1pt/575ml malt vinegar

To peel the tomatoes plunge them in hot water for a few seconds and skins will come away easily.

Mix all vegetables together and put into large saucepan. Add sugar, chillies, sultanas, chopped garlic, ginger and vinegar. Bring to the boil, turn down heat and leave to simmer for about one and half hours until thick, soft and brown, stirring frequently. Pour mixture into dry sterilised jars. Cover with jam covers, then with a round cloth, brush with melted candle grease to ensure an air-tight seal.

Ideal accompaniment to cold meat, cheese or curry.

Recommended variety - Bramley

GREEN TOMATO AND APPLE CHUTNEY - 2

1lb/450g green or red tomatoes (peeled - see recipe 1 - and chopped)
1lb/450g sharp cooking apples
1 large onion (peeled and chopped)
4 cloves garlic (crushed)
2 tablespoons raisins
4 prunes (seeded and chopped)
12ozs/350g brown sugar
1 tablespoon salt
12fl.oz/325ml wine or cider vinegar
1 teaspoon ground ginger and allspice

Put all the above ingredients in a large heavy based saucepan. Bring to the boil and simmer very gently for over an hour until the mixture has the consistency of jam, stir often as it begins to thicken and become sticky. Add a pinch of cayenne pepper towards the end of the cooking time if you like it hot.

Allow to cool before putting into dry sterilised jars.

Recommended variety - Bramley

TOMATO, APPLE AND PEPPER CHUTNEY

4lbs/1.8kg ripe tomatoes (skinned and halved)
4 green peppers (discard seeds and chop remainder)
Grated rind of 2 small oranges
Grated rind and juice of 2 lemons
Half pint/275ml white malt vinegar
5oz/150g soft brown sugar
1¹/₂oz/40g sea salt
1 teaspoon gound black pepper
1 teaspoon ground mace
1 teaspoon ground ginger
4 sharp tasting eating apples (peeled, cored and chopped)

Put the tomato seeds in a sieve and rub them with a wooden spoon to extract all their juice. Put the tomato halves, peppers and tomato juice into a large preserving pan and add the remaining ingredients ensuring the apples are freshly chopped and have not discoloured. Stir well and bring the mixture slowly to the boil and simmer until it is rich and thick (about 1¹/₂-2hrs). Put chutney into jars but do not secure tops until it is quite cold.

Recommended variety - Bramley

MARROW AND APPLE CHUTNEY

2lbs/900g well-ripened marrow (cut into 1"/2.5cm cubes)
4lbs/1.8kg apples (peeled, cored and chopped)
6lbs/2.6kg sugar
8oz/225g onions or shallots (chopped)
8oz/225g raisins
1½oz/40g salt
Cayenne pepper
Ground ginger
1oz/25g citric or tartaric acid
Three quarters pint/425ml vinegar

Put the apples, onions, raisins and sugar into a large preserving pan and boil
until the apples are almost pulped, stir mixture continuously. Add the the
marrow and continue to simmer mixture until the marrow is transparent and
the apples are pulped. Add the salt, pepper and ginger to taste, citric acid and
vinegar and continue to simmer for a further 15 minutes. Allow mixture to cool
slightly and then pour into hot sterlized jars. Seal when cold.

Recommended variety - Bramleys

APPLE CURD

8oz/225g margarine
2lb/900g apples (peeled, cored and chopped)
2 eggs
8oz/225g sugar
Juice of 1 lemon

Boil apples until pulpy. Add the sugar and melted margarine and then beat in
the two eggs. Cook slowly for half an hour, add the lemon juice and the pot in
jars in the usual way. Will keep for about two months.

Recommended variety - Golden Noble

APPLE GINGER

4lb/1.8kg apples (peeled, cored and cut into thin slices)
3pt/1700ml water
4lb/1.8kg sugar
2oz/50g ground ginger (or according to taste)

Make a thick syrup by boiling the sugar and water together in a preserving pan.
Add the apples and boil until apple is transparent, add the ginger and boil for a
further five minutes. Put in warm sterilized jars and cover.

Recommended variety - Golden Russets are best but others will do

APPLE GINGER JAM (makes 5 x 16oz/450g jars)

3lb/1.4kg cooking apples (peeled, cored and thinly sliced)
1pt/575ml water
Grated peel and juice of 2 lemons
1 teaspoon ground ginger
3lb/1.4kg sugar
4oz/100g chopped crystallized ginger

Put apples, water, lemon peel and juice and ground ginger in a large pan and
simmer until the apples are soft. Add the sugar and stir until it is dissolved.
Increase heat and boil rapidly for 15-20 minutes or until jam reaches
105C/221F. Remove from heat and stir in the crystallized ginger.
Skim off scum and leave to stand
for 5-10 minutes. Pot in hot sterilized jars and cover.

Recommended variety - Blenheim Orange

APPLE JELLY - 1

10lbs/4.5kgs crab apples or cooking apples with a strong flavour (peeled, cored and sliced)
5 pints/3 litres water
4-6lbs/1.8-2.7kgs sugar
3 lemons

When slicing a large quantity of apples to prevent them browning, it is recommended they are placed in a basin of cold salted water and a plate put over slices to keep them below the surface. Before cooking rinse the sliced apples in cold water.

Put in large heavy based pan, tie peel and cores (these contain the pectin to make the jelly) in muslin and add to the apples in the pan. Cover with water and cook on a brisk heat until tender, adding the juice of three lemons. When fruit is cooked pass it through a sieve and let it drain for about two hours. Measure the quantity of apple mixture remaining and allow the same quantity of sugar. Put pan back on heat with the apples and sugar and let it boil for quarter of an hour, stirring constantly, as long as the sugar is not completely melted. The jelly is ready when a drop of the juice sets on the spoon which has been dipped in it. Put into dry, warmed sterilised jars.

Recommended varieties - see above

APPLE JELLY - 2

Apples (washed and cut up) - see recipe for quantities
1lb/450g sugar per 1pt/575ml apple juice

Put apples in a large pan and add a little water. Bring to the boil and then simmer for one hour, add more water if necessary. Strain mixture, weigh and return to preserving pan adding 1lb/450g sugar for every 1pt/575ml of apple juice. Boil mixture rapidly until setting point is reached. Pot in the usual way.

Recommended variety - Bramley/Dumelow's Seedling

APPLE MARMALADE

6lb/2.7kg apple pulp from the Apple Jelly
6lb/2.7kg sugar
2 lemons
Cinnamon

Pass the pulp through a fine sieve, add the lemon juice, sugar and cinnamon. Put in a heavy based pan and boil for 5 minutes. Put into jars (as on next page).

GREEN TOMATO AND APPLE MARMALADE

1lb/450g tomatoes (sliced thinly)
1lb/450g apples (peeled, cored and cut into small chunks)
1¼lb/550g granulated sugar
2 tablespoons/30ml vinegar
2 tablespoons/30ml water

Place apples and tomatoes in a large earthenware bowl. Add the sugar, vinegar and water, stir well with a wooden spoon and leave for a day or two, stirring occasionally. It should become syrupy. Turn into a preserving pan and bring to the boil. Boil for about 40 minutes or until the apple become transparent. Put in warmed sterlized jars and cover. Keep for a while before using.

Recommended variety - Bramley

APPLE AND PLUM JELLY

3lbs/1.35kg dessert apples (peeled, cored and chopped)
3lbs/1.35kg tart plums (stoned and sliced)
1pt/575ml cold water
Juice of 2 lemons
2lbs/900g sugar

Put fruit and water into heavy-based preserving pan, bring to boil and simmer until soft. Stir in lemon juice and strain pulp through a jelly bag overnight. Measure quantity of juice and allow 1lb/450g sugar to every 1pt/575ml of juice. Heat juice over a low heat and stir in sugar until it has dissolved. Bring to the boil until setting point. Ladle into warmed sterilised jars, cover with a waxed disc, seal and label.

Recommended varieties - Cox/Worcester Pearmain/Katy

APPLE AND BLACKBERRY JAM - 1

3¹/₂lb/1.35kg apples (peeled, cored and sliced thinly)
2lb/900g blackberries
3¹/₂lb/1.35kg sugar

Put apples into preserving pan with 8fl.oz/225ml water and allow to simmer until the apples are tender. Add blackberries, boil together for 5 minutes and then add the sugar. Bring to the boil and boil fast for 25-30 minutes. Pot in warm sterilized jars and cover.

Recommended variety - windfalls will do

APPLE AND BLACKBERRY JAM - 2

1lb/450g apples (weight when peeled, cored and sliced)
1lb/450g blackberries (washed)
2lb/900g sugar
2 tablespoons/30ml water

Simmer apples gently in the water until soft. Add the blackberries to the apple mixture and heat gently until the fruit is soft. Stir in the sugar, continue to heat gently and stir until the sugar is dissolved. Then boil rapidly until setting point is reached. Pot in warm sterilized jars and cover.

Recommended variety - Lord Derby/Bramley

APPLE AND APRICOT JAM

1lb/450g dried apricots (cut into small pieces and soaked in 1pt/575ml water)
12lb/5.5kg apples (washed and cut up, but not peeled)
1lb/450g sugar per 1pt/575ml cooked pulp
Water

Boil apples in sufficient water to ensure thorough cooking. Strain cooked apples squeezing through all the pulp. Drain the apricots, add to the apples and weigh final mixture. For each pint/575ml of pulp add 1lb/450g sugar and stir well. Boil mixture fast and test for setting, stirring frequently. When ready put into warm sterilized jars and cover.

Recommended variety - windfalls will do

APPLE & BLACKBERRY JELLY

3lbs/1.35kg blackberries
2pts/1200mls water
3lbs/1.35kgs cooking apples (washed and thinly sliced but not peeled or cored)
Sugar - allow 1lb/450g per 1pt/575mls of strained apple mixture)

Place fruit in large pan with water and simmer gently until soft (about 1½ hours). Strain cooked mixture through a jelly bag (several layers of muslin or fine woven cotton will do). Allow to drip and do not press fruit. (Helpful tip - if you scald the jelly bag with boiling water before using it speeds up the dripping process). The test for pectin by putting 3 teaspoons of methylated spirits in a small jar, add 1 teaspoon of the mixture and swirl it around. If a good clot is obtained the juice is ready for the next process; if a poor clot, boil further to remove excess moisture and test again.

Measure juice and allow 1lb/450g sugar to each one pint/575mls of juice.

Put clean jars and sugar in a warm oven.

Heat the strained juice in a clean pan and stir in the warmed sugar, dissolving before bringing to the boil. Have a thermometer ready in hot water. Boil jelly rapidly but do not stir. Put in thermometer and when it registers 220F remove pan from heat, skim away any scum and pot at once in the warmed jars. Place waxed discs to cover surface. Do not use very large jars.

Recommended variety - Lord Derby/Bramley

APPLE, DATE AND WALNUT CHUTNEY

1lb/450g onions (peeled and chopped)
2lb/900g cooking apples (peeled, cored and chopped)
1¹/₂lb/675g dates (stoned and chopped)
3oz/75g chopped walnuts
1 pint/575ml vinegar
1 teaspoon salt
1 teaspoon ground ginger
1 teaspoon/5g Cayenne pepper
8oz/225g sugar

Place onions in large heavy based pan with a little water. Bring to the boil and simmer until soft. Add the apples and continue cooking gently for 15-20 minutes. Add dates, walnuts, salt, spices and half the vinegar. Cook, stirring occasionally, until the mixture thickens. Add the sugar and remaining vinegar and stir until all the sugar has been dissolved. Continue to simmer until the chutney becomes really thick and stir occasionally. Put into dry warmed sterilised jars and seal. Use after 2-3 weeks.

Recommended varieties - Bramley

WINDFALL CHUTNEY (this recipe makes about 9-10lb/4.1-4.5kg chutney)

2¹/₂lbs/1.1kg windfall apples (peeled, cored and chopped)
2¹/₂lbs/1.1kg windfall pears (peeled, cored and chopped)
2¹/₂lbs/1.1kg windfall plums (stoned)
2lbs/900g onions (peeled and chopped)
2lbs/900g green tomatoes (washed and quartered)
8oz/225g mixed seedless raisins and sultanas
1lb/450g marrow flesh (cut into 1.5cm cubes)
1¹/₂pints/850ml malt vinegar
2oz/50g whole mixed pickling spice (tied in a muslin bag)
8oz/225g soft brown sugar
2oz/50g salt

When preparing fruit cut away all bruised or damaged flesh leaving sound fruit in half inch/1¹/₂cm chunks. Place prepared fruit in a large heavy based pan with the chopped onions, tomatoes, dried fruit and marrow flesh. Add half the vinegar and the spices in the muslin bag. Bring to the boil and then simmer gently until tender and pulpy, stir occasionally.

Add the sugar, salt and remaining vinegar and stir until all the sugar dissolves. Continue cooking gently, stirring occasionally, until chutney becomes thick. Remove the bag of spices and put chutney into dry warmed jars. Seal and leave to mature for 4-6 weeks.

Recommended varieties - all kinds

SPICED APPLE BUTTER (makes about 4-5 1lb/450g jars)

4lbs/1.8kgs crab apples (halved)
2pints/1.1litre water
1 tablespoon whole cloves
2 chips nutmeg
2 x 2"/5cm pieces of cinnamon stick
2½lbs/1.125kgs (approx) dark brown sugar

Place halved crab apples in a large heavy based preserving pan with the water, cloves, nutmeg and cinnamon sticks. Bring to the boil and simmer, stirring occasionally, for about one hour. The mixture should then be ready to beat into a thick pulp.

Put the pulp through the fine blade of a vegetable mill and then weigh it. Return it to the cleaned pan and stir in 12oz/350g sugar to every 1lb/450g of the apple purée. Put the pan on a low heat and stir until the sugar dissolves. Bring to the boil and keep boiling, stirring frequently, until the butter is very thick. If you draw a wooden spoon through it, it should leave a channel behind it. This may take up to one hour.

Put the butter into warmed sterilised preserving jars and cover tightly while it is still hot. The butter is ready for use as soon as it is cooled. Store butter in a refrigerator once you have opened a jar.

Recommended variety - Veitch's Scarlet

APPLE BUTTER - 1 (makes about 6lbs/2.8kg)

3lbs/1.4kg cooking apples (washed and chopped without peeling or coring)
1³/4pt/1litre water
3lb/1.4kg light raw brown sugar
Half teaspoon ground cinnamon (optional)
Half teaspoon ground cloves (optional)

Place apples in preserving pan, cover with water and simmer gently until pulpy. Sieve and weigh the pulp and return it to the pan. Add ³/4lb/450g of sugar to every 1lb/450g of apple pulp. Add the spices, if wanted. Heat gently, stirring occasionally until the sugar is dissolved, then boil until mixture becomes thick and creamy. Pour into hot, sterilized jars and seal with jam pot covers.

Recommended variety - Bramley

APPLE BUTTER - 2

3lbs/1.4kg crab apples or windfalls (washed and chopped but not peeled or cored)
1pt/575ml cider or apple wine (if not available use half pint/275ml water)
Granulated sugar (³/4lb/340g to every 1lb/450g of apple pulp)
Half teaspoon powdered cinnamon
Half teaspoon ground cloves

Place chopped apples in pan with liquid, cover and simmer until soft. Sieve and weigh the pulp, return it to the cleaned pan and simmer a little longer to allow it to thicken. Add the sugar and spices and leave mixture to simmer until a spoon drawn across it leaves its own impression. Pot mixture immediately into hot, sterlized jars and put waxed discs to cover surface. When quite cool put on tops and store in a cool, dark place.

Recommended variety - any cooker/Veitch's Scarlet/John Downie

APPLE & GINGER CHUTNEY - 1 (makes about 4lbs/2kg)

1¼pt/700ml cider vinegar
1½lb/675g raw brown sugar
Half ounce/14g pickling spice (tied in small piece of muslin)
2¼lb/1kg cooking apples (cored and chopped)
8oz/225g onions (skinned and chopped)
4oz/100g root ginger (peeled and grated)
1oz/25g garlic cloves (crushed)
1oz/25g salt
4oz/100g sultanas

Heat the vinegar and sugar slowly in a large saucepan until the sugar is dissolved. Add all the prepared ingredients to the pan with the pickling spice in muslin. Bring the mixture to the boil, reduce heat and simmer, stirring occasionally for about 2 hours, or until it is thick and no thin liquid remains. Remove the pickling spice. Pour the chutney into hot sterilized jars and cover with vinegar-proof paper.

Recommended variety - Bramley

APPLE GINGER CHUTNEY - 2 (makes 3lbs/1.4kg)

3lb/1.4kg cooking apples (peeled, cored and chopped finely)
12oz/350g light brown sugar
1pt/575ml cider vinegar
1½ tablespoons salt
1½ teaspoons ground ginger
1 teaspoon ground allspice
1 teaspoon ground cloves
1 green pepper (chopped finely)
1 medium onion (chopped finely)
4oz/100g preserved ginger (finely chopped) in syrup
4oz/100g sultanas
Grated peel and juice of half a lemon

Put apples, sugar, vinegar, salt and spice in large saucepan and bring to the boil, stirring well. Reduce heat and allow to simmer for 10 minutes. Add the pepper, onion, ginger and syrup, sultanas, lemon peel and juice. Bring mixture back to the boil and then reduce heat. Simmer for one hour or until thick and golden brown. Stir occasionally. Ladle chutney into hot, sterilized jars, wipe clean and cover. Allow chutney to mature for one month before using.

Recommended variety - Bramley

BLACKBERRY AND APPLE CHUTNEY

2lb/900g blackberries
12oz/350g onion (rough chopped)
1pt/575ml white vinegar
2 teaspoons/10ml ground ginger
Half ounce/14g dry mustard
2lb/900g cooking apples (peeled, cored and rough chopped)
1lb/450g brown sugar
3 teaspoons salt
1 teaspoon ground mace

Put all the ingredients with the exception of the sugar into a preserving pan and mix well. Bring to the boil and simmer for about an hour. If the blackberry pips are disliked the mixture can be sieved at this point. Add the sugar to the mixture, stir until dissolved and bring to the boil. Continue cooking until the mixture is quite thick and all the vinegar has been absorbed. Pot into warm sterilized jars and seal while hot.

Recommended variety - Lord Derby/Bramley

PLOUGHMANS PICKLE

2lb/900g turnips (peeled and cut into very small cubes)
1lb/450g onions (peeled and chopped)
8oz/225g dark brown sugar
Half ounce/14g turmeric
2oz/50g salt
1lb/450g apples (peeled, cored and chopped)
8oz/225g raisins
1 teaspoon dry mustard powder
A little freshly ground pepper
2pt/1.1litre malt vinegar

Boil turnips in salted water until soft and drain well. Put the cooked turnips, onion, apples, raisins, sugar, salt and pepper into a large pan. Mix the turmeric and mustard to a thin paste with the vinegar and add to the other ingredients. Bring to the boil and simmer slowly for about an hour, stirring frequently to avoid sticking. Put into warm sterilized jars and cover while warm. Leave for about two weeks to mature.

Recommended variety - Golden Noble

APPLE CHUTNEY - 1

4¹/₂lb/2kg apples (peeled, cored and chopped)
¹/₂lb/675g sultanas
pt/575ml brown vinegar
1lb/450g soft dark brown sugar
4oz/100g salt
1oz/25g mustard seed
Three quarters ounce/20g grated ginger
1oz/25g garlic (finely chopped)
Quarter ounce/7g Cayenne pepper

Boil the apples, sultanas and vinegar in a large preserving pan until the mixture is pulpy and leave to cool completely. Add all the remaining ingredients and leave for three days, stirring once a day. Put into dry sterilized jars and seal.

Recommended variety - any

APPLE CHUTNEY - 2

2lb/900g apples (peeled, cored and chopped)
1lb/450g sultanas
Half ounce/14g mustard seed
Pinch of Cayenne pepper
8oz/225g onions (peeled and chopped)
1¹/₂lb/675g brown sugar
Quarter tablespoon salt
Half ounce/14g whole ginger
1¹/₂pt/850ml vinegar

Put apples and onions into preserving pan with vinegar, sugar, sultanas and pepper with the mustard seeds and ginger tied in a muslin bag. Simmer until the vegetables are tender and the mixture has slightly thickened. Remove the muslin bag, put chutney into warmed sterilized jars and cover.

Recommended variety - any

APPLE CHUTNEY - (3)

4lb/1.8kg apples (cored and chopped)
2lb/900g onions (peeled and chopped)
8oz/225g sugar
8oz/225g sultanas or finely chopped dates
1 tablespoon salt
Pinch of Cayenne pepper
1pt/575ml spiced vinegar

Put all the ingredients into a pan sprinkling over with the salt and pepper and cover with the spiced vinegar. Bring to the boil and simmer gently for 2 hours, stirring frequently. Put into warmed sterilized jars and cover tightly.

Recommended variety - windfalls are suitable

APPLE CHUTNEY - 4

3lb/1350g apples (peeled, cored and sliced)
1¹/2lb/675g onions (chopped)
1¹/2lb/675g demerara sugar
1 tablespoon salt
1 teaspoon ground ginger
1 teaspoon mixed spice
Half teaspoon white pepper
1lb/450g sultanas
1pt/575ml vinegar

Put all the ingredients into a large preserving pan, bring to the boil and simmer briskly for one hour, stirring frequently. Pot into warm sterilized jars and seal.

Recommended variety - Bramley

ROAST APPLE CHUTNEY

6 large cooking apples
Beetroot juice
2 shallots (finely chopped)
1 tablespoon/15ml chili vinegar
Dash of Cayenne pepper and salt

Roast apples until they are soft then mash them to a pulp. Colour them red with the beetroot juice. Put into a large pan and add the shallots, chili vinegar, pepper and salt. Simmer mixture very gently until it resembles thick cream. Bottle in warm sterilized jars and seal.

Recommended variety - Bramley

RAW APPLE RELISH (makes about 1pt/575ml)

3 sharp tasting apples
1 green pepper
1 sweet red pepper
1 onion
2 stalks celery and tops
3 tablespoons/45ml honey
3 tablespoons/45ml lemon juice
lemon rind

Grind all the ingredients together and serve relish with cold red or white meat or fish.

Recommended variety - Cox/Bramley

COOKED CRANBERRY AND APPLE RELISH (makes 2pts/1 litre)

1lb/450g cranberries
8fl.oz/225ml sweet cider
2 sharp tasting apples (sliced but not peeled)
8fl.oz/225ml honey
Grated lemon rind
Pinch of ground mace

Gently simmer the cranberries, cider and apples until fruit is soft. Add the honey, lemon rind and mace and simmer for 5 minutes. Cool mixture and serve with red or white meat or fish.

Recommended variety - Bramley/Granny Smith

MINCEMEAT - 1

1lb/450g apples (peeled, cored and finely chopped)
Half ounce/14g butter
8oz/225g currants
8oz/225g raisins
8oz/225g sultanas
4oz/100g candied peel
4oz/100g dates (chopped small)
8oz/225g soft brown sugar
6oz/175 grated suet
Grated rind and juice of 1 lemon
1 teaspoon cinnamon
Half teaspoon grated nutmeg
4 tablespoons/60ml rum

Melt butter in pan, add the apple and cook gently until it has softened. Leave to cool completely.

Put the cooked apple and the remaining ingredients in a large bowl and mix well together. Cover and leave in the bowl for 24 hours, stirring occasionally. Put mincemeat into cold sterilized jars, leaving a space at the top. Put on a waxed paper disc and cover with pot covers. Store in a cool, dry, dark place.

NB. By cooking the apple this helps to keep the mincemeat longer; raw apple tends to make it ferment after a few weeks.

Recommended variety - Bramley

MINCEMEAT - 2 (makes about 3 x 1lb/450g jars)

1/2lb/225g apples (peeled, cored and minced)
4oz/100g each of sultanas, raising and currants
4oz/100g chopped mixed peel
2oz/50g chopped glace cherries
4oz/100g finely shredded suet
Grated rind and juice of 1 orange
Grated rind and juice of 1 lemon
6oz/175g demerara sugar
1 teaspoon mixed spice
3 tablespoons/45ml whisky

Mince apples with the fruit and peel and mix in the other ingredients well.
Bottle and seal in sterilized jars.

Recommended variety - Bramley

GOLDEN APPLE MINCEMEAT

2lb/900g sweet apples (peeled, cored and diced)
1 1/2lb/675g sugar
Juice of 1 lemon
1 teaspoon ratafia essence
4oz/100g lemon peel (shredded)
2lb/900g sultanas
1 teaspoon ground ginger
Half teaspoon mace
1pt/575ml water

Butter bottom of a preserving pan and put in the apples, sultanas and water.
Cook gently for 20 minutes. Mix the spices into the sugar, add the lemon juice
and lemon peel and stir into the apple mixture. Boil for a further 20 minutes.
Allow to cool, then stir in the ratafia essence. Pot in small sterilized jars and
cover.

Recommended variety - Pippins/Cox/King of Pippins

DRIED APPLE RINGS

Firm, ripe apples (peeled, cored and thickly sliced rings)
2 tablespoons salt
4½pt/2.65litres water

Set oven at 110C/225F/Gas Mark ¼.

Add salt to water to make brine and immerse apple rings in solution. Leave to stand for 10 minutes, drain and thread on to wooden skewers.

Place skewers on oven shelves so apple rings are not touching and leave in oven for 4-5 hours or until rings resemble soft leather and are moist and pliable. Remove from oven and leave to stand for 12 hours. Store in airtight containers in a cool dry place.

To use, soak in fresh water for 24 hours, then place in a saucepan and cook apples and liquid over a low heat with a few strips of lemon peel, vanilla pod or a pinch of ground cloves.

Recommended variety - any as available

APPLE CANDY

6 large cooking apples (baked)
8oz/225g sugar (use more if not sweet enough)
1 egg white

Remove skins from baked apples and pass through a sieve. Then add the sugar, beating well. Add the white of an egg, beaten in well.

Cover a board with a linen cloth and spread the apple purée over it about half an inch/1cm thick. Leave overnight in a half warm oven (as for dried apple rings) and cut into squares the next day. Powder with sugar and store in an airtight container.

Recommended variety - Bramley

MIXED FRUIT CHUTNEY

2 or 3 each of apples, plums, pears, apricots, peaches (cored, stoned, peeled and cut into small pieces)
For every 2lb/900g fruit allow the following:-
2oz/50g sultanas
12oz/300g sugar
8fl.oz/225ml cider or wine vinegar
1-2 teaspoons garam masala
8 large cloves of garlic (crushed)
Quarter ounce/7g salt
1 teaspoon groud ginger, chilli or Cayenne to taste

Put all ingredients into a large pan, bring to the boil and simmer gently for at least 45 minutes, stirring frequently until mixture is soft, sticky and thickened. Allow to cool before bottling in sterilized jars.

Recommended variety - Conference/Concorde

PEARS IN RED OR WHITE WINE

2lb/900g small hard pears (peeled, leaving stalks on)
1 bottle red or white wine
1lb/450g sugar
4/5 cloves (optional)
Stick of cinnamon (optional)
Rind of 1 lemon (optional)

Put ingredients in a large pan and simmer for about 45 minutes or until tender. Transfer pears to a large jar. Reduce the syrup by boiling fast and pour over pears. If desired add a few tablespoons of pear brandy or a fruit liqueur such as cassis.

Serve pears with cream, yoghurt or cream cheese.

Other fruit such as halved peaches, sour cherries or apple slices may be similarly prepared.

Recommended variety - Gorham/Glou Morceau/Conference

PICKLED PEARS

7lb/3kg stewing or hard pears (peeled and halved and covered with cold water to prevent discolouration)
3lb8oz/1.5kg sugar
Juice and grated rind of 1 large lemon
Half pint/275ml white vinegar
Half ounce/14g root ginger (bruised)
A few cloves

Put all ingredients except the pears into a large pan and boil for two minutes. Add the pears and boil until tender. Keep lid on the pan to retain steam until sufficient liquid covers the pears. Put into warmed, sterilized bottles and tie tops securely.

Recommended variety - Conference/Concorde/Gorham

PEAR AND PINEAPPLE CONSERVE

2lb/900g pears (peeled, cored and thinly sliced)
8fl.oz/225ml water
1lb/450g sugar
1 small pineapple, peeled and coarsely grated

Allow 5 8oz/225g jars. These should be washed in hot soapy water, rinsed and kept warmed until needed.

Put pears, water and sugar in a large pan and bring to the boil. Add the pineapple and simmer for 45 minutes. Ladle the hot conserve into the warmed jars, wipe thoroughly with a clean cloth and seal.

Recommended variety - Conference

PEARS MULLED IN RED WINE

6lb/2.75kg small unripe pears (peeled but left whole retaining stalks)
1lb/450g sugar
1 lemon (peel cut into thin strips)
1 bottle red wine
1 teaspoon whole cloves
1 cinnamon stick cut into sufficient pieces to allow 1 per jar
4 blades of mace
2 x 3"/8cm pieces of root ginger (bruised)
Water

Set oven at 130C/250F/Gas Mark 1/2.

Wash jars as for conserve allowing about 6 x 1lb/450g jars.

Pack the pears into the prepared jars and divide sugar evenly. Place a strip of lemon peel in each jar, and divide evenly between the jars the cloves, cinnamon stick, mace blades and ginger. Pour wine over the pears and top up jars with water.
Put tops on jars but not the screwbands. Place in the oven for 3 hours.
Remove and screw tops on tightly. Cool and store.

Recommended variety - Conference/Gorham

PEAR AND PEACH JAM

2lb/900g ripe pears (peeled, cored and chopped; put cores in a muslin bag)
1lb8oz/675g peaches (peeled, sliced and stoned)
5fl.oz/150ml water
3lb/1350g sugar
Grated peel and juice of 3 lemons

Prepare 5 x 1lb/450g jars as above, keeping warmed until needed.

Put pears, muslin bag, peaches and water in a large pan and bring to the boil. Reduce heat and simmer until fruit is soft. Remove muslin bag. Add sugar, lemon peel and juice and stir until sugar dissolves. Increase heat and boil rapidly for 15-20 minutes or until jam reaches 105C/221F. Remove from heat, skim off scum and leave to cool for 5-10 minutes. Ladle jam into prepared jars, wipe and seal.

Recommended variety - Williams/Comice/Conference

PEAR JAM - 1

10lb/4.5kg pears (peeled, quartered and cored)
7lb8oz/3.5kg caster sugar
2pt/1.1litre water

Boil pears in water for 3 minutes and drain. Make a syrup with the sugar and water and when it is boiling add the pears. Allow to cook for about an hour. Ladle into prepared jars and seal.

Recommended variety - Conference/Comice/Concorde

PEAR JAM - 2

To every 2lb/900g pears allow 1lb/450g caster sugar and finely grated rind of 1 lemon.

Peel, quarter and core the fruit, put in a basin, layering pears and sugar, cover and leave to stand for 24 hours. Then transfer to a pan and bring to the boil quickly, stirring constantly. Add the lemon rind 10 minutes before the jam is ready. Put into warmed clean jars, leave to cool and seal. Store in a cool place.

Recommended variety - Conference/Comice/Concorde

PEAR PASTE

4lb/1.8kg pears (peeled, cored and quartered)
1pt/575ml water
4lb/1.8kg sugar

Cook pears slowly in the water and when cooked press through a fine sieve. Weigh this sieved fruit, add the same weight of sugar and place in a pan. Heat again, stirring continuously until mixture becomes very thick and looks like paste and does not stick to the pan. Lightly grease some flat moulds and sprinkle with caster sugar. Put paste in these moulds and leave in the oven overnight on a very low heat. Allow to cool. Sprinkle caster sugar on a cool board and turn out the paste. Cut up into lozenges, sprinkling over more sugar, and store in tins.

Recommended variety - Comice/Conference

PRESERVED PEARS IN SYRUP

10lb/4.5kg pears (peeled)
3lb/1350g sugar
3pt/1800ml water

When peeling the pears keep in a light brine, under the surface to prevent discolouration. Remove pears from water, drain and dip in boiling water for one minute and then quickly in cold water. Place fruit in clean sterilised jars. Make the syrup with the sugar and water by bringing to the boil and boiling fast for one minute. Pour over the fruit in the jars, leave to cool and seal.

Recommended variety - Comice/Concorde

PRESRVED PEARS IN BRANDY SYRUP

Quantities and method as above but add half pint/275ml brandy to the syrup before pouring over the prepared pears.

Recommended variety - Gorham/Conference/Concorde